THE GREEK TRAGEDY
IN NEW TRANSLATION

GENERAL EDITORS
Peter Burian and Alan Shapiro

SOPHOCLES: Philoctetes

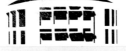

MALIS: The district of Greece just south of Thessaly. Its name means "Sheepland."

MENELAOS: Son of Atreus, brother of Agamemnon, and husband of Helen.

THE MOTHER: An Anatolian goddess, whose cult is associated with Mt. Ida and Troy. Cybele was the Mother of the Gods and in Greek tradition Rhea, the mother of Zeus.

MYCENAE: The city of Agamemnon in Argos.

NESTOR: King of Pylos, who took part in the Greek expedition against Troy, accompanied by his son Antilochos, who died there.

ODYSSEUS: Son of Laertes (or Sisyphos) and Antikleia, King of Ithaca.

OITA: A high mountain in southern Thessaly. Its summit was the site of Herakles' pyre and cult.

OLYMPOS: The highest mountain in Thessaly, the seat of the gods and of divine Herakles.

PAKTOLOS: An river in Lydia with deposits of gold flowing south of Sardis.

PATROKLOS: Close companion of Achilles, killed in by Apollo and the Trojan Euphorbus as he took to the field in Achilles' armor.

PHILOCTETES: From Malis in Thessaly, son of Poias, and an archer in possession of the bow of Herakles.

PHOINIX: The old tutor of Achilles.

POIAS: Of Malis, father of Philoctetes.

PREPARETHOS: Now Skopelos in the Sporades, an island to the south and west of Lemnos.

PYLOS: A city in the southwest Peloponnesus and center of the kingdom of Nestor.

SIGEION: A city on the coast of the Troad and the place where Achilles was buried.

SISYPHOS: Reputedly the father of Odysseus. He attempted to deceive the gods and return to the earth from Hades and was punished for this attempt by the frustrated task of rolling a stone up a hill in the Underworld.

SKYROS: A small island in the Sporades and the birthplace of Neoptolemos.

SPARTA: The city of Menelaos in Laconia.

SPERCHEIOS: The major river of the plain of Malis.

TEUCER: The son of Telamon and younger brother of Ajax. He was a skilled archer.

THERSITES: The ugliest of the Achaean army who spoke out against Agamemnon in assembly.

THESEUS: King of Athens in the generation before the Trojan War. His sons Akamas and Damophon were part of a fictive embassy to Philoctetes on Lemnos.

TROY: The city of Laomedon and Priam in Phrygia, whose walls were built by Poseidon and Apollo. First attacked by Herakles, Telamon, and Philoctetes; then by the army of the Atreidai. It was destroyed in the tenth year of that war.

TYDEUS: Father of Diomedes.

ZEUS: Son of Kronos and Rhea, the paramount god of the Greek pantheon.

SOPHOCLES

Philoctetes

Translated by
CARL PHILLIPS
With Introduction and Notes by
DISKIN CLAY

OXFORD
UNIVERSITY PRESS

2003

OXFORD
UNIVERSITY PRESS

Oxford   New York
Auckland   Bangkok   Buenos Aires   Cape Town   Chennai
Dar es Salaam   Delhi   Hong Kong   Istanbul   Karachi   Kolkata
Kuala Lumpur   Madrid   Melbourne   Mexico City   Mumbai   Nairobi
São Paulo   Shanghai   Taipei   Tokyo   Toronto

Copyright © 2003 by Oxford University Press, Inc.

Published by Oxford University Press, Inc.
198 Madison Avenue, New York, New York 10016

www.oup.com

Oxford is a registered trademark of Oxford University Press

Library of Congress Cataloging-in-Publication Data
Sophocles.
[Philoctetes. English]
Philoctetes / Sophocles ; translated by Carl Phillips ;
with introduction and notes by Diskin Clay.
p.   cm.—(The Greek tragedy in new translations)
ISBN-13 978-0-19-513657-9
1. Philoctetes (Greek mythology)—Drama.   2. Trojan War—Drama.
I. Title: Sophocles—Philoctetes.   II. Phillips, Carl, 1959–
III. Clay, Diskin.   IV. Title.   V. Series.
PA4414.P5 P48   2003
882'.01—dc21
2002032763

9 8 7 6 5 4
Printed in the United States of America

EDITORS' FOREWORD

"*The Greek Tragedy in New Translations* is based on the conviction that poets like Aeschylus, Sophocles, and Euripides can only be properly rendered by translators who are themselves poets. Scholars may, it is true, produce useful and perceptive versions. But our most urgent present need is for a *re-creation* of these plays—as though they had been written, freshly and greatly, by masters fully at home in the English of our own times."

With these words, the late William Arrowsmith announced the purpose of this series, and we intend to honor that purpose. As was true of most of the volumes that began to appear in the 1970s—first under Arrowsmith's editorship, later in association with Herbert Golder—those for which we bear editorial responsibility are products of close collaboration between poets and scholars. We believe (as Arrowsmith did) that the skills of both are required for the difficult and delicate task of transplanting these magnificent specimens of another culture into the soil of our own place and time, to do justice both to their deep differences from our patterns of thought and expression and to their palpable closeness to our most intimate concerns. Above all, we are eager to offer contemporary readers dramatic poems that convey as vividly and directly as possible the splendor of language, the complexity of image and idea, and the intensity of emotion of the originals. This entails, among much else, the recognition that the tragedies were meant for performance—as scripts for actors—to be sung and danced as well as spoken. It demands writing of inventiveness, clarity, musicality, and dramatic power. By such standards we ask that these translations be judged.

This series is also distinguished by its recognition of the need of nonspecialist readers for a critical introduction informed by the best recent scholarship, but written clearly and without condescension.

Each play is followed by notes designed not only to elucidate obscure references but also to mediate the conventions of the Athenian stage as well as those features of the Greek text that might otherwise go unnoticed. The notes are supplemented by a glossary of mythical and geographical terms that should make it possible to read the play without turning elsewhere for basic information. Stage directions are sufficiently ample to aid readers in imagining the action as they read. Our fondest hope, of course, is that these versions will be staged not only in the minds of their readers but also in the theaters to which, after so many centuries, they still belong.

A NOTE ON THE SERIES FORMAT

A series such as this requires a consistent format. Different translators, with individual voices and approaches to the material in hand, cannot be expected to develop a single coherent style for each of the three tragedians, much less make clear to modern readers that, despite the differences among the tragedians themselves, the plays share many conventions and a generic, or period, style. But they can at least share a common format and provide similar forms of guidance to the reader.

1. *Spelling of Greek names*

Orthography is one area of difference among the translations that requires a brief explanation. Historically, it has been common practice to use Latinized forms of Greek names when bringing them into English. Thus, for example, Oedipus (not Oidipous) and Clytemnestra (not Klutaimestra) are customary in English. Recently, however, many translators have moved toward more precise transliteration, which has the advantage of presenting the names as both Greek and new, instead of Roman and neoclassical importations into English. In the case of so familiar a name as Oedipus, however, transliteration risks the appearance of pedantry or affectation. And in any case, perfect consistency cannot be expected in such matters. Readers will feel the same discomfort with "Athenai" as the chief city of Greece as they would with "Platon" as the author of the *Republic*.

The earlier volumes in this series adopted as a rule a "mixed" orthography in accordance with the considerations outlined above. The most familiar names retain their Latinate forms, the rest are transliterated;–*os* rather than Latin–*us* is adopted for the termination of masculine names, and Greek diphthongs (such as Iphigen*ei*a for Latin Iphigenia) are retained. Some of the later volumes continue this practice, but where translators have preferred to use a more consistent practice of transliteration or Latinization, we have honored their wishes.

2. Stage directions

The ancient manuscripts of the Greek plays do not supply stage directions (though the ancient commentators often provide information relevant to staging, delivery, "blocking," etc.). Hence stage directions must be inferred from words and situations and our knowledge of Greek theatrical conventions. At best this is a ticklish and uncertain procedure. But it is surely preferable that good stage directions should be provided by the translator than that readers should be left to their own devices in visualizing action, gesture, and spectacle. Ancient tragedy was austere and "distanced" by means of masks, which means that the reader must not expect the detailed intimacy ("He shrugs and turns wearily away," "She speaks with deliberate slowness, as though to emphasize the point," etc.) that characterizes stage directions in modern naturalistic drama.

3. Numbering of lines

For the convenience of the reader who may wish to check the translation against the original, or vice versa, the lines have been numbered according to both the Greek and English texts. The lines of the translation have been numbered in multiples of ten, and those numbers have been set in the right-hand margin. The (inclusive) Greek numeration will be found bracketed at the top of the page. The Notes that follow the text have been keyed to both numerations, the line numbers of the translation in **bold**, followed by the Greek line numbers in regular type, and the same convention is used for all references to specific passages (of the translated plays only) in both the Notes and the Introduction.

Readers will doubtless note that in many plays the English lines outnumber the Greek, but they should not therefore conclude that the translator has been unduly prolix. In some cases the reason is simply that the translator has adopted the free-flowing norms of modern Anglo-American prosody, with its brief-breath- and emphasis-determined lines, and its habit of indicating cadence and caesuras by line length and setting rather than by conventional punctuation. Even where translators have preferred to cast dialogue in more regular five-beat or six-beat lines, the greater compactness of Greek diction is likely to result in a substantial disparity in Greek and English numerations.

Durham, N.C.
Chapel Hill, N.C.
2003

PETER BURIAN
ALAN SHAPIRO

CONTENTS

PHILOCTETES

INTRODUCTION

THE LEGEND AT THE EDGES OF THE ILIAD

The wrath of Achilles, directed first at Agamemnon and then at the Trojan who killed his friend Patroklos in battle, begins with the first line of the *Iliad* and ends with the last. In its stark simplicity, this wrath is the story of the *Iliad*, which opens with Homer's appeal to the Muse, "Sing goddess, of the wrath of Achilles, the son of Peleus" and ends with these words: "And so they carried out the burial of Hector, breaker of horses." The legend of the archer from Malis who will arrive at Troy only after the deaths of Hector and Achilles lies on the penumbra of the *Iliad*. Philoctetes' fate in the epic of Ilion is perfectly matched by his ten-year isolation on the island of Lemnos, where he was abandoned as the Achaians crossed the northern Aegean to make their assault on Troy. This legend, which is located at both edges of the *Iliad*, is the subject of Sophocles' *Philoctetes*.

Philoctetes is recalled near the beginning of the *Iliad* in the Catalogue of Ships (*Iliad* 2.716–28). His contingent of seven ships is said to have been manned by archers from Methone, Thaumakia, Meliboia, and rough Olizon—places that are only names to us now. His force of 450 men comes under the command of a subordinate named Medon when Philoctetes is abandoned on the "divine island of Lemnos"—"in the pain and anguish of the brutal bite of the snake that intended his death." Philoctetes remained on Lemnos as his comrades battled on the plain of Troy, "but soon memory of Lord Philoctetes would return to the minds of the Achaians" (*Iliad* 2.716–20). Homer's description of Philoctetes' state of mind on Lemnos, where he "sat in anger and in

In the Introduction and Notes, the line numbers in boldface refer the reader to this translation; the following line numbers refer to the Greek text of Sir Hugh Lloyd-Jones and N. G. Wilson, *Sophoclis Fabulae*, Oxford 1990.

grief," echoes what he had just said of Achilles, as he had withdrawn to his ships from the Greek army in anger and resentment (*Iliad* 2.694). Both warriors will be sorely missed by the Achaians (*Iliad* 1.240 of Achilles).

Apparently, what made the Achaian army on the plains of Troy think of a comrade who had been left on Lemnos for ten long years does not need to be explained to Homer's audience. It requires some explanation for the reader of Sophocles' *Philoctetes*. Philoctetes' history is situated on the edges of the Homeric epics. There is a great deal of epic history that Homer excluded from his *Iliad*. He only glances at the antecedents of the Trojan War in the fateful choice offered to Paris by three rival goddesses, Hera, Athena, and Aphrodite, at the end of the epic (*Iliad* 24.25–30). Priam is king of Troy when the forces of Agamemnon reach the Troad, but Homer can take his audience back to the antecedents of Priam's kingship in Dardanos (as recalled by Aeneas in *Iliad* 20.215–41 and 304–5).

The Greek tragedians are more attentive to the events that followed the conclusion of Homer's *Iliad*. When they choose to write of the history of Troy, they concentrate on the events that took place in the interval between the death of Hector and the capture of Troy; and then on the fate of the Trojans who survived the destruction of their city. The traditions that lay on the periphery of the *Iliad* were known in antiquity as "The Epic Cycle," and Sophocles was said to have been attracted to this fascinating and unHomeric poetry.[1] Aeschylus wrote a play, much appreciated by ancient readers (including Sophocles), on the award of the arms and armor of Achilles after the "best of the Achaians" was killed by the arrow Paris aimed at his heel. His *The Decision over the Arms* [of Achilles] might be reflected in the episode we find in Sophocles' *Philoctetes*; one of the invented complaints Achilles' son, Neoptolmos, adduces to explain to Philoctetes his disaffection with the Greek army is the decision of the army to award the arms of his father to Odysseus (*Philoctetes* 360–76/359–81). Sophocles' *Ajax* is the dramatization of the rage and frustration of Ajax, who, after Achilles, could claim the coveted title "best of the Achaians" (*Iliad* 2.768–69), but saw the award of the arms go to the guile and eloquence of Odysseus.

1. Acording to the learned Athenaeus of Naucratis in Egypt, "Sophocles was delighted by the Epic Cycle and composed entire plays that closely followed its plots," Deipnosophistai 7.277C. Accessible accounts of the Epic Cycle can be found in G. L. Huxley, *Greek Epic Poetry from Eumelos to Panyassis* (London 1969), 123–61, and Malcolm Davies, *The Greek Epic Cycle*, second edition (London 2001).

After Achilles falls to Paris' arrow, the forces that bring about the destruction of Troy combine in rapid succession. In the anticipations to be found in Sophocles' play the events of this legend unfold in four stages: Odysseus manages to capture the Trojan seer, Helenos, who had unwisely left Troy at night. The seer is brought before the Greek army and forced by Odysseus to reveal that Troy will not fall until Philoctetes brings his bow from Lemnos and Achilles' son comes to Troy from Skyros (*Philoctetes* 603–21/614–25 and 1332–42/1329–47); persuaded by Herakles, Philoctetes arrives at Troy, with the bow of Herakles, which will spell the doom of Paris. Before he goes into action, his wound is healed by Machaon and Podaleirios, the two physicians who serve the Greek army—or by Asklepios himself; finally, he and Achilles' son join together to take Troy (*Philoctetes* 1490–1511/1329–47 and 1614–32/1418–40). In Sophocles' version of this part of the Troy tale, Neoptolemos is as necessary to the capture of the city his father could not take as are Philoctetes and the bow of Herakles. This combination of events might be termed "double determination." But, in this case, the determination does not involve the combination of divine and human forces as it often does in the *Iliad*; it involves two warriors whose legends are situated on the edges of the *Iliad*.

There is one crucial condition for the fall of Troy not mentioned in the *Philoctetes*. This is Odysseus' strategem of the wooden horse left for the Trojans by the departing Greeks as an offering to Athena. In the *Odyssey*, Odysseus tells Achilles that Neoptolemos had entered the Trojan horse with him and conducted himself bravely (*Odyssey* 11.523–32). The omission of any mention of the strategem of the Trojan horse seems a deliberate slight to Odysseus.

The actual capture and sack of Troy is the matter of post-Homeric epics; it is not the matter of the tragic poets of Athens in the last three decades of the fifth century.[2] What happened after the capture of Troy was the subject of three of the surviving plays of Euripides. He treats the fate of the women of Troy and the killing of Astyanax, the son of Hector and Andromache, in his *Trojan Women* (produced in 415), a play that ends with the certainty of the imminent destruction of the city of Troy. The fate of widowed Hecuba (who in the *Trojan Women* is awarded as part of the plunder of Troy to Odysseus) and her son Polydoros is the subject of his *Hecuba*; and his *Andromache* takes Hector's widow (awarded to Neoptolemos in *Trojan Women*) to Greece as a concubine of the son of the man who murdered her husband. In

---

2. Sophocles wrote a *Philoctetes at Troy*; only reports of it survive.

Euripides' *Andromache*, Pyrrhos (as Neoptolemos is called here) has none of the inherited nobility of the Neoptolemos of Sophocles' *Philoctetes*.[3]

The tragic legend of Philoctetes is, then, situated at the edges of Homer's *Iliad* and in some ways frames it. Philoctetes is the only Greek warrior to take part in the two Greek expeditions against Troy: in the first expedition against the city of Laomedon he is accompanied by Herakles and Telamon, father of Ajax. He takes no part in the action of the *Iliad*, which is intensely concentrated on the plain of Troy during a period of four days of combat and one day of truce in the tenth year of the siege. The legend of Philoctetes, as it connects with the second expedition against Troy, begins with his receiving the bow and arrows that will be fatal to Paris and to Troy from Herakles on Mt. Oita, the mountain that rises to the south of the plain of Malis—a mountain often mentioned in Sophocles' play—both as the rugged symbol of his home and the place of Herakles' immolation (682–89/664–70). In Sophocles' play it is Philoctetes who consented to put a torch to Herakles' pyre; he received in gratitude the bow given to him by Herakles. Consumed by the poison daubed on the shirt of the centaur Nessos gave Herakles' wife Deianera and she gave her husband, Herakles will serve as the model for the sufferings of Philoctetes on Lemnos (*Philoctetes* 1607–13/1417–25). In the scenes exhibiting the intense pain of the two heroes, the *Philoctetes* is a pained echo of Herakles in the *Women of Trachis*.

Philoctetes has a close relation to Herakles; he had served him as both stopped to sacrifice at the sanctuary of Chryse on the small island of that name that once lay off the coast to the east of Lemnos.[4] This was at the beginning of the first Greek expedition against Troy and Herakles' assault on the city of Laomedon. It is finally Herakles who persuades the adamantly resentful Philoctetes to sail to Troy with the hated Odysseus and the young warrior who had returned his bow to him (*Philoctetes* 1598–1646/1419–51). When he is finally cured by the physicians of the Greek army on the Troad and has helped capture Troy with the bow of

3. Interestingly, the club house (*lesche*) of the Knidians above the temple of Apollo at Delphi contained Polygnotos' version of the sack of Troy on its right wall. Neoptolemos, who was said to be buried nearby, evidently played a major role in this pictorial narrative, as is clear from the description Pausanias gives in his *Description of Greece*, 10.25–26. Polygnotos painted the lesche in the fifties of the fifth century; his painting survived until the time of Pausanias in the mid-second century A.D. It is Apollo who is responsible for the murder of Pyrrhos at Delphi (Euripides, *Andromache* 1161–65).

4. A bell crater now in Vienna shows the richly clad statue of the goddess surmounting a column placed behind an altar where Herakles is about to sacrifice, illustrated in Figure 2 of "Chryse I," *Lexicon Iconographicum Mythologiae Classicae* III.2 (Zurich and Berlin 1986).

Herakles, Philoctetes is instructed to deposit some of the spoils from Troy in the sanctuary of Herakles on Mt. Oita as a memorial to the divine power of Herakles' bow (*Philoctetes* 1620–24/1429–33).

Philoctetes' knowledge of the location of the island and sanctuary of Chryse was essential to the Achaian armada, as the Greeks made a second expedition against Troy. Sacrifice to Chryse was, apparently, necessary for their reaching Troy (as was sacrifice to Artemis at Aulis, as the fleet left the Greek mainland). It was at this sanctuary that Philoctetes was bitten by the snake that guarded the place. The agony and loathsome suppuration from this poisonous wound to Philoctetes' foot caused the Greek army—and Odysseus as their agent—to abandon him on Lemnos. He was to remain on the island Sophocles makes uninhabited and desolate during the siege of Troy, until the frustrated Greek army sends Odysseus and Neoptolemos to persuade him—or force him—to come, with his bow, to Troy. Sophocles' play opens as Odysseus and Neoptolemos have arrived on Lemnos and approach the seaside cave that has been Philoctetes' shelter; it ends as Herakles appears at one of the two mouths of Philoctetes' cave to resolve the human impasse and seal the fate of Priam's Troy (1598/1409). The words of Herakles, now a divine resident on Mt. Olympos, persuade Philoctetes to accompany Odysseus and Neoptolemos back to Troy. No strategem of Odysseus or noble appeal of the son of Achilles or the chorus can bring this about. The irreconcilable conflict between two opposed worlds of value prompts Sophocles to adopt the Euripidean device of introducing a deus ex machina to break the human impasse.

LEMNOS

We begin on Lemnos. Lemnos was populated long before the destruction of Troy (if Schliemann's Troy VI is Priam's city). The coastal site of Polichni belongs to the Late Bronze Age (1500–1000 B.C.). For Homer, Lemnos had close associations with Hephaistos (because of its vulcanism) and was populated. When Zeus hurled Hephaistos down onto Lemnos—Milton's "th' Aegean isle"—he is cared for by a people called the Sinties (*Iliad* 1.590–94). In the *Odyssey* (8.294), the Sinties are described as speaking like animals, and Homer has Hephaistos returning from Olympos to "the strong city of Lemnos" (*Odyssey* 8.284–85). It is remarkable that Sophocles, who wrote his *Philoctetes* after Aeschylus and Euripides had written theirs, should make Lemnos a bleak, uninhabited island and thus leave Philoctetes there in a state of utter isolation. The isolation of Philoctetes on Lemnos is only one of the salient differences between the earlier Philoctetes plays of Aeschylus and Euripides and Sophocles' play. Euripides gives Philoctetes a Lemnian companion by the name of Aktor. In 431 (the date of Euripides' *Philo-ctetes*) there should have been nothing unusual about Lemnians as companions to the outcast Philoctetes; in 450 the Athenians had sent a group of colonists (cleruchs) out to the island to secure control of the seaways to Thrace and up into the Black Sea. Its two principal cities Myrrhine and Hephaistia were important Athenian settlements, and Athena of Lemnos was worshipped on the acropolis of Athens. A cult of Chryse seems to have been located near the Pnyx in Athens. There was also an important Athenian cult of Herakles on the island. Lemnos was well populated at the date of Sophocles' *Philoctetes*.

As the play opens, Odysseus and Neoptolemos have landed on Lemnos in search of Philoctetes. They find no trace of humans on the Lemnian shore, only the cave of Philoctetes above them, with its two openings. The foul rags that Philoctetes uses to bandage his wound are the only signs of the island's single human inhabitant; they are visible on the rocky side of the cave. The term that most often describes Philoctetes in Sophocles' play is *eremos*—alone, isolated, companionless. But finally, he will be true to his name (a combination of *philos*, "friend," and the verb *ktasthai*, "to possess") as he finds a true friend in the young Neoptolemos.

As the sailors from Skyros first encounter him, it is clear to them that Philoctetes has become savage (220–21/225–26 and 1479/1321). His "bed" is made of leaves (41/33); his "roof" of rock (1400/1262). His food is described as fodder (*phorba*, 49/43 and 1221/1107)—a word for the food of beasts. He lives by his bow, and the association of bow (*biós*) and life (*biós*) is latent in Sophocles' Greek. The few visitors who are driven to the island refuse to take Philoctetes with them, leaving him once again with no human contact (503–7/494–96). And, when he finally readies to leave the island, Philoctetes invokes the world of nature that has become so familiar to him (1647–71/1452–68), as he had in his long lyric invocation of the life he would lead on Lemnos without his bow (1200–79/1081–1162):

> I . . . call upon this island . . . ,
> chamber that kept watch over me,
>
> water-nymphs,
>
> nymphs of the meadows,
>
> the muscled crashing of sea against headland,
> where often my head, though
> inside the cave, was drenched by the south wind's beating,
> and often the mountain of Hermes sent
> back to me in answer
> my own voice

echoing,
groaning,
as I weathered the storm.

But now,
o streams and Lycian spring,
we take leave of you—I leave you
at last. . . .

Farewell, Lemnos, surrounded by sea.

This is the passage that inspired in Matthew Arnold "the eternal note of sadness" as he stood on Dover Beach:

Sophocles long ago
Heard it on the Ægæan, and it brought
Into his mind the turbid ebb and flow
Of human misery.[5]

PHILOCTETES BEFORE PHILOCTETES

Of all the tragedies produced in Athens in the competitions of the festivals of Dionysos only seven survive of Aeschylus, seven of Sophocles, and eighteen of Euripides. (Each year three tragic poets competed with three tragedies and a satyr play in the festival of the Greater Dionysia.) By good luck, we can compare the distinctively different talents of the three great Athenian tragedians as they dealt with the theme of Orestes and Electra and their revenge on their mother, Clytaemnestra, for the treacherous murder of their father, Agamemnon. In the unique case of Aeschylus' *Choephoroi* (*Libation Bearers*), Sophocles' grim *Electra*, and Euripides' realistic play of the same title, we have a sequence of three extant plays treating the same subject written over nearly half a century (from 458 to approximately 413). In a sense, these plays are "trilogies" in that we can see the three tragic poets whose works have survived in dialogue. In them, we can attend to the silent dialogue of Sophocles with Aeschylus, and of Euripides with both Aeschylus and Sophocles. Euripides' staging of the scene in which Electra recognizes her brother can only be fully appreciated as a sophisticated reenactment of the same scene in Aeschylus' *Choephoroi* (*Electra* 508–52; *Choephoroi* 154–211).

We cannot directly assess the very different dramatic thought and art of the three tragedians in the treatment of any other theme. But Dio of Prusa could. In the late first century or early second century of the imperial period, Dio's library in Prusa contained the Philoctetes plays of Aeschylus, Euripides, and Sophocles. To exercise his mind, he spent a day reading the plays and wrote (and must have delivered in public)

---

5. There is also the striking description of Oedipus as a promontory battered by the sea in Sophocles' last play, *Oedipus at Colonus* 1240–48.

a comparison of the three tragedies. These three Philoctetes plays were never entered in competition one against the others, and Dio possessed the refinement not to decide on the superiority of one poet over the others. Yet, as a skilled and erudite public speaker (*sophistes*), he was clearly attracted to Euripides' treatment of the character of Odysseus, who was for the Greeks the archetype of the sophist and demagogue — and, then, of the successful orator of Dio's age (Speech 52). Indeed, Dio gives a prose version of the Prologue and first Episode of Euripides' *Philoctetes* (Speech 59).

Sophocles' *Philoctetes* won first prize at the competitions of the greater Dionysia of 409. We know that Euripides entered his *Medea* and *Philoctetes* in the competitions of 431 (and won third prize). As readers of Sophocles' *Philoctetes*, we face the unusual sequence of Aeschylus, Euripides, and then, after an interval of twenty-two years, Sophocles. (We do not know the date of Aeschylus' play.) Dio takes up the discussion of the three Philoctetes plays in this order. As we will see, there are signs in Sophocles of the impact of the dramatic art of Euripides. His *Philoctetes* is his only extant play whose intractable human conflict is resolved by a deus ex machina. The god who appears — not from the machine, but on the upper ledge of the cave above Philoctetes' cave — is Herakles.

Although Sophocles' *Philoctetes* comes last in sequence, Dio places Sophocles between the extremes of Aeschylus' rugged grandeur and Euripides' admirable — and highly imitable — rhetorical agility; he is "intermediate" (*mesos*) (Speech 52 §15). This is Sophocles' position in the dramatic contest between Aeschylus and Euripides in Aristophanes' *Frogs*, a play produced in 405, two years after the death of Euripides and the year after the death of Sophocles. Standing between the two extreme representatives of Attic tragedy, Sophocles is described as "easygoing in Hades and easy-going on earth" (*Frogs* 82; cf. 787).

But in his treatment of the Philoctetes legend, Sophocles stands at an extreme. To assess the distinctive shape of his *Philoctetes*, Sophocles' reader — and ancient audience — must place his play in a context larger than a recognition of the two Philoctetes plays that preceded his in the Theater of Dionysos. When it was first produced, Aeschylus' *Philoctetes* did not enter into dialogue with an earlier play; Euripides' *Philoctetes* is not merely a dialogue with Aeschylus; and Sophocles' *Philoctetes* is not merely the third play in Dio's trilogy. Although Philoctetes is mentioned only three times in the Homeric epics,[6] and plays no role in the

---

6. We have seen him in the Catalogue of Ships, *Iliad* 2.716–28. He is mentioned again in the *Odyssey*, as the greatest archer of the Greek army (8.219) and as having safely reached home, unlike Odysseus (3.190).

action of the *Iliad*, Sophocles' characterization of Philoctetes' stubborn and archaic heroism is informed by Sophocles' deep understanding of the extremes of heroic character represented by Homer's Achilles and Odysseus. Sophocles also knew and could appreciate infinitely better than can we the post-Homeric epics that dealt with his theme. He had prepared for his *Philoctetes* by producing his *Ajax* and *The Women of Trachis*. He also wrote *The Madness of Odysseus*, a *Phoinix*, *The Islanders of Skyros*, and *Philoctetes at Troy*—all now vanished with little trace.[7] As important, Sophocles also knew the political culture of Athens during the period of the Peloponnesian War, a period that saw the sudden and dramatic influence of the sophistic movement in the Athenian political assemblies, law courts, and theater. One of the most important of the Athenian sophists was Euripides.

We have already observed how Sophocles also departs from both Aeschylus and Euripides in depopulating the island of Lemnos. The Prologue to his play opens with Odysseus' description of the island:

This coast—

This shore—

This is Lemnos, the sea surrounds it. No man
lives here—even steps here.

It is clear from Dio that the chorus of both Aeschylus and Euripides was made up of Lemnians (Speech 52 §7). By contrast, Sophocles provides the abandoned warrior with no human companionship: only the sea, the grey rocks, and the birds, and animals that provide Philoctetes with his livelihood. None of the occasional visitors who are forced to land on the island are willing to take Philoctetes off it (300–314/303–13); Philoctetes is forced to ask some of the departing visitors to take a message to his father (503–7/494–96).

The effect of Philoctetes' isolation in Sophocles' play is twofold: it makes the great archer, who possesses the formidable bow of Herakles, as savage and elemental as the island he inhabits, a place of rugged cliffs, raging surf, air pierced with the cry of birds, and the fire of Hephaistos. His isolation also makes Philoctetes a throwback to a vanished heroic past and at the same time the object of pity for Neoptolemos and his Skyrians. The other way in which Sophocles reshapes

---

7. They can be appreciated in the Loeb edition of Sir Hugh Lloyd-Jones, *Sophocles*, vol. 3, Fragments (London 1996).

the tragic myth of Philoctetes is that he adds Neoptolemos to the embassy of Odysseus. The result is that the young son of Achilles is caught in the tension between his loyalty to Odysseus and the Greek army at Troy and his admiration and sympathy for the hero who represents the values and stubbornness of the father he never knew. In this sense, Philoctetes is no longer isolated once Odysseus and Neoptolemos land on Lemnos. He comes to occupy an extreme, and the young Neoptolemos is caught between the powerful forces of Odysseus and Philoctetes.

DRAMATIS PERSONAE

Aristotle spoke epigrammatically of Sophocles' contribution to the development of Attic tragedy: "the third actor and scene painting."[8] In Greek tragedy at the time of Sophocles' *Philoctetes* the speaking parts were divided among three actors: the protagonist (first actor), deuteragonist (second actor), and tritagonist (third actor). In the case of his *Philoctetes*, a single actor plays the parts of Neoptolemos and Philoctetes, but the versatile actor who plays the part of Odysseus also plays the part of the Trader (548–641/542–627) and of Herakles at the end of the play (1598–1638/1409–68). This actor is—to employ the Homeric epithet that describes Odysseus in the first line of the *Odyssey*—*polytropos*, a man of many turns.

No character in a Greek tragedy stands in isolation; conflict and contrast are essential to drama and characterization. This is true of the Homeric epics. The case of Odysseus is instructive. In the *Iliad*, Menelaos is described as being taller than Odysseus when both stand before the Greek army; but, when both are seated, Odysseus is the more majestic figure. As a speaker, Menelaos' delivery is rapid; he does not use many words and his voice is clear. When Odysseus comes to address the assembly, he leaps to his feet and then stands stock still with his eyes fixed on the ground as rigidly as the scepter he holds motionless in his hand. He seems a dolt. But, when he begins to speak, he speaks with a strong voice and his words fall on the ears of his audience like great flakes of snow. Such is the Trojan Antenor's description of Odysseus (*Iliad* 3.204–24). In the case of Odysseus, unlike any other Homeric hero, appearances are deceiving. Helen confirms Antenor's description as she identifies Odysseus to Priam from the walls of Troy: "This the crafty son of Laertes, Odysseus, who was raised on Ithaca, a

---

8. *Poetics* 4.1449ᵃ 18.

rocky place to grow up in. He knows many twists, and turns, and clever strategems" (*Iliad* 3.191–202).

Odysseus is the most fully described character in the Homeric poems, not only because he manages to survive the *Iliad* to become the hero of the *Odyssey*. His wit, eloquence, and guile combined with his prudent but conspicuous bravery make him unique among Homeric heroes. But, as Antenor's description makes clear, Odysseus' character cannot be understood in isolation; it is revealed in a system of meaningful contrasts.[9] In his *Philoctetes*, Sophocles creates a tension between Odysseus and Philoctetes that, like Philoctetes' bow, is never relaxed. This tension is so intense that Odysseus cannot at first face the suffering warrior he was commanded to abandon on Lemnos. The young[10] Neoptolemos is caught between these two antagonists, who represent not only the conflict between authority and Philoctetes' deeply injured pride, but a conflict between the heroism—if heroism is the word for it—of adaptability and cunning and the fixity of the blunt, archaic heroism of Philoctetes. Odysseus is prudently unwilling to get within range of Philoctetes' bow; Philoctetes is imprudently willing to let himself be caught in the net of lies Odysseus throws over him. The world in which Odysseus lives and moves so deftly is the world of Athens of 409, when eloquence was, in the words of the sophist Gorgias, a "great potentate"[11] in every public arena. This was a world split between words (*logoi*) and reality (*erga*); it was a world in which speech became reality. In contrast to the versatile Odysseus, who moves on and off stage, and whose deeds are words, Philoctetes is virtually immobile because of his injured leg. His language is often reduced to inarticulate cries of agony, and his hatred of the Atreidai and their agent Odysseus is as inveterate and incurable as his wound.

No dramatic detail makes the vanished world of stolid heroism and the contemporary world of agile sophistry more apparent than the interview of Neoptolemos with Philoctetes, who has had no word of the fate of the warriors who had been his companions as far as Lemnos on their way to Troy. Here Sophocles rehearses the dramatic scene from the Underworld in which Odysseus sights the great warriors who died on the plains of Troy and interviews Agamemnon Achilles, and attempts to get a response from Ajax (*Philoctetes* **403–37**/403–36; *Odyssey*

9. As when Priam notes that he is shorter than Agamemnon by a head (*Iliad* 3.193).
10. By sober chronology, Neoptolemos, who is often addressed as "child" (*pais*), would be about ten at the time of the embassy to Lemnos. He is usually presented as about eighteen or an ephebe.
11. So described by Gorgias in his display piece, *In Praise of Helen* § 8 in Hermann Diels and Walther Kranz, *Die Fragmente der Vorsokratiker* (Berlin 1952) 82 B 10. See note to line 145.

11.387–564). Ajax, Neoptolemos tells Philoctetes, is dead. It is Ajax who, after Achilles, was recognized as "the best of the Achaians."[12] Nestor lives on, but in grief for the loss of his son Antilochos, who fell at Troy. Patroklos too is enlisted in the nation of the glorious dead. But the sons of Atreus, Diomedes, and Odysseus still live on: "War" Neoptolemos says, "will always prefer those who are most noble" (437/436–37).

Philoctetes now asks about "a worthless creature, but clever and a skilled speaker." Neoptolemos is puzzled for a moment and hesitates: "Whom do you mean, if not Odysseus?" (441/438–41) The worthless creature Philoctetes had in mind is in fact not Odysseus, but Thersites. It is a measure of Odysseus' rapid decline in the age of Sophocles that the son of Achilles should think of Odysseus and not Thersites, notorious in the *Iliad* for his comic ugliness and abusive and incoherent speeches before the Greek army at Troy. Thersites is hated by both Achilles and Odysseus (*Iliad* 2.211–42). In this episode of the *Iliad*, it is Odysseus, the upholder of authority, who beats the upstart Thersites with the gold scepter that is the emblem of Agamemnon's kingly authority, to the universal approval of the assembly (*Iliad* 2.243–77). Yet Homer admits that this, the worst of the Achaians, is an appealing speaker (*Iliad* 2.246).

Recalling his interview with the soul of Ajax in the Underworld, Odysseus claims that not only the Achaians but Athena awarded him the arms of Achilles (*Odyssey* 11.547). Athena suggests guile; her particular attachment to Odysseus is motivated by the intelligence they both share in common. In his *Ajax*, Sophocles had handled the theme of the consequences of the award of the arms of Achilles (and implicitly his title as "the best of the Achaians") to Odysseus and not to Ajax. Sophocles' *Ajax* resembles his *Philoctetes* in one crucial feature: both plays dramatize the injured pride of a warrior who has been disgraced by Odysseus and the sons of Atreus; and in both the shamed and injured warrior becomes isolated from his society. And, in a sense, Sophocles stages a contest over the divine bow of Herakles in his *Philoctetes*. Character does not carry over from Homer to the tragedians or from one tragedy to another, but it is worth noting that Ajax's contempt for Odysseus and the sons of Atreus is matched by Philoctetes' contempt for Odysseus and his commanders. In the earlier play, when he has regained his sanity, Ajax calls Odysseus "the most fawning, dangerous, and despicable sharper" (*Ajax* 955–60).

12. Both in the Catalogue of Ships (*Iliad* 2.768) and in the judgment of his mortal enemy Odysseus, who attempts to speak with him in the Underworld (*Odyssey* 11.469–70).

In Sophocles' *Philoctetes*, Neoptolemos is a new presence on the stage of the theater of Dionysos. It appears that Sophocles invented the part of Neoptolemos in the embassy to Philoctetes; in Euripides' *Philoctetes*, Odysseus' companion was Diomedes.[13] The young son of Achilles is caught and vacillates between the extremes of human values represented by Odysseus and Philoctetes. When Odysseus cajoles him to play his part in deceiving Philoctetes and bringing him aboard their ship, he flatters him by addressing him as the son of Achilles and tells him "you'll have to be as noble as your birth is" (57/51). Neoptolemos' response to Odysseus' appeal to play this role "for a brief, shameless part of the day" (94/83) is predictable: "Son of Laertes, I hate doing things that are painful even to listen to" (97/86–87). He is reenacting the part of his father and displaying his inherited genius. His words recall those his father addressed to Odysseus.

Neoptolemos' reply and the embassy of Odysseus to Lemnos subtly recall an earlier embassy from the *Iliad*, that sent by Agamemnon to the tent of Achilles on the shore of Troy. In *Iliad* 9 (122–61), Agamemnon lists for Odysseus, Ajax, and Phoinix the gifts he will give Achilles to persuade him to relent in his anger and return to battle against Troy. He ends by saying that Achilles should give way to him, "in as much as I am more kingly than he and older than he in years" (160–61). When he comes to the tent of Achilles, Odysseus repeats Agamemnon's offer, but diplomatically omits his last injunction. Achilles could not have heard what Agamemnon had said, but his response seems to be directed against Odysseus as well as Agamemnon, whom he mistrusts: "Zeus-born Odysseus, son of Laertes, man of many shifts. . . . More than I hate the gates of Hades I hate the man who says one thing and conceals another in his heart!" (308–13). He has a similar response to Odysseus' suave flattery as they meet in Hades (*Odyssey* 11.467–91).

In his initial reaction to Odysseus' proposal, Neoptolemos plays the part of his father. But he relents and plays the part Odysseus has assigned to him for just about half the play. What turns him away from his false role in Odysseus' plot to capture Philoctetes is the sight of Philoctetes' bow: "And what is it you're holding now — is *that* the famed bow?" (669–70/654). Now begins what William Arrowsmith has called "the sacrament of the bow."[14] In entrusting this "sacred" bow to the young son of Achilles, Philoctetes has enacted the meaning of his name

---

13. As is clear from Dio's description of the play, *Speech* 52 §14.

14. In an unpublished lecture given at Hope College in 1976. I am grateful to Stephen Esposito for making a transcript of this lecture (which I heard Arrowsmith deliver on Martha's Vineyard in June 1977) available to me. It is entitled "Heroism and the 'sacrament of the bow' in Sophocles' *Philoctetes*."

and acquired a friend. It is precisely at this point of the play that Neoptolemos and the confederate chorus of his subjects stop acting their roles in Odysseus' cunning plot and come to pity the atrocious suffering of the owner of the bow. Despite Odysseus' threat of violence (1390/1254–55), Neoptolemos is determined to return the bow to its rightful owner. He will not make a tool of Philoctetes or separate him from his bow. After three frustrated attempts to leave Philoctetes' cave for their ship and return to Skyros and Malis, Neoptolemos and Philoctetes join forces to face the threat of violence from the Greek army. Philoctetes will protect Neoptolemos and Skyros "with the arrows of Herakles" (1593/1406). At these words Herakles appears. In an uncanny way, the seemingly mismatched solidarity of Philoctetes and Neoptolemos recalls the revenge Odysseus takes on the suitors in the *Odyssey*, with the bow given him by Iphitos and his young son by his side.

The conflict of Sophocles' *Philoctetes* has no solution. The words of the chorus that open Seamus Heaney's *The Cure at Troy* recognize the human impasse.[15]

> Philoctetes.
>   Hercules.
>   Odysseus.
> Heroes. Victims. Gods and human beings.
> All throwing shapes, every one of them
> Convinced he's in the right, all of them glad
> To repeat themselves and their every last mistake,
> No matter what.

DRAMATURGY

The Play within the Play
In the *Philoctetes*, Sophocles' dramatic art is invested in characterization, the plots devised by Odysseus that mimic his own larger construction, his use of a conspiratorial chorus, the stage property of the talismanic bow, sudden entrances and a long delayed exit, and the final deus ex machina that seems to settle all that is left in suspense and assure the Troy tale of its expected ending. Sophocles' dramatization of the mission of Odysseus and Neoptolemos to bring Philoctetes from Lemnos to Troy is, as we have seen, inspired by the embassy of Odysseus, Ajax, and Phoinix to the tent of Achilles in *Iliad* 9. This embassy can be sighted just behind the stage of Sophocles' play. Within the play, there are three fictive embassies that are an integral part of the

---

15. *The Cure at Troy: A Version of Sophocles' Philoctetes* (New York 1991).

plot of the play; they are all part of Odysseus' plot to capture Philoctetes and his bow by guile. They are introduced by Odysseus who rehearses for Neoptolemos the lying tale he is to tell Philoctetes about the insult of the award of the arms of his father to Odysseus by the Greek army (63–76/55–69). Even at the end of the play, Neoptolemos cannot reveal to Philoctetes that he was lying about the arms (1532–39/1362–66).

The prelude to Odysseus' lying tale has Neoptolemos arrive at the Troad to discover that the arms of his father had been awarded to Odysseus, who, when reproached, had the audacity to reproach the young Neoptolemos for not being at Troy when he was needed (380–81/379–80). In his own shame and anger Neoptolemos does what Achilles only threatened to do (first in *Iliad* 1.169–71): sail back home. This, in the plot of Odysseus' play, is the insult that brings Neoptolemos to Lemnos on his way home to Skyros. It is a tale designed to elicit the sympathy and confidence of Philoctetes, who had been disgracefully treated by both the Atreidai and Odysseus, "that worst of all evil men" as Neoptolemos describes him on cue (385/384; cf. 73–74/64–51).

The first fictive embassy of the *Philoctetes* is the embassy of Odysseus and Phoinix, the tutor of Achilles, to bring Neoptolemos from Skyros to Troy (341–53/343–53); it is the prelude of the mission of Odysseus and Neoptolemos to Lemnos. A part of what Neoptolemos tells Philoctetes about this mission reflects the legend of the fall of Troy, but it includes an Odyssean accent of deception. According to Neoptolemos, Odysseus and Phoinix managed to persuade him to come to Troy by claiming that, with Achilles dead, *only* his son could take Troy. This contradicts the oracle Herakles delivers at the end of the play: Neoptolemos and Philoctetes were *both* needed to finally capture the city (1625–29/1433–37). The oracle of Helenos that the Trader repeats to Neoptolemos and Philoctetes also contradicts the oracle of Herakles: according to the Trader, Philoctetes *alone* was needed for the capture of Troy (622–25/610–13). Neoptolemos and the Trader both play their assigned parts in Odysseus' drama staged on Lemnos with skill.

The second fictive embassy is announced to Neoptolemos and Philoctetes by the Trader. His role is played by the actor, who also plays the role of Odysseus. The Trader arrives on the scene with one of Neoptolemos' sailors just as Neoptolemos had promised to take Philoctetes off the island (548/542). His tale is that he too has come from Troy and, finding Neoptolemos on Lemnos, can warn him of a new "plot" of the Argives against the already outraged boy. An embassy made up of "old Phoinix" and the sons of Theseus is on its way to Skyros. Neoptolemos asks the relevant question: "To bring me back by violence, or with words?" (567/563). Philoctetes will ask the same question.

What explains the absence of Odysseus on such a mission is the fact that he was sent with Diomedes (his companion in the Doloneia of the *Iliad*) on still another mission to bring Philoctetes to Troy. This is the third false embassy. The Trader feigns that he does not quite know who Philoctetes is as he announces their quarry (578–79/573). Him they will bring to Troy either by force or persuasion.

The plot of Odysseus' play on Lemnos in which Neoptolemos, the chorus, and the "Trader" all play their assigned parts, is well described by Odysseus as a "clever strategem" (*sophisma* in Greek 20/14). It is cunningly contrived to accomplish its ends by words and it plays effectively on the pride that Odysseus and the Atreidai had mortally wounded. The last of the lying embassies rehearsed by the Trader casts both Neoptolemos and Philoctetes as the quarry of the Greek who had insulted them: Philoctetes in truth and Neoptolemos in Odysseus' fiction. No force can drive Philoctetes onto Neoptolemos' ship and deliver him to Troy; although Odysseus once offers to use force (1075/983), he relies on words and, like Sophocles, produces his own play within a play.

The Complicit Chorus

The chorus of the *Philoctetes* are subjects of Neoptolemos from the island of Skyros. (In this they resemble the chorus of Sophocles' *Ajax*, which is made up of sailors from Salamis.) They have accompanied Neoptolemos from Skyros to Troy and have now come to Lemnos in the mission to bring Philoctetes to Troy. There are two striking features of Sophocles' use of the chorus in the *Philoctetes*: the lyrical portions of the play are severely reduced when compared to the other plays of Sophocles (including his last play, *Oedipus at Colonus*); the chorus enter into the action of the play with more involvement in its plot than any other Sophoclean play.

It is not clear from the language of the play when the chorus of the *Philoctetes* enters the orchestra. They might appear after Odysseus and Neoptolemos have made their entry on stage. Certainly they have assembled before the audience sometime before they speak. As participants in the action—and the plot—of the *Philoctetes*, they are closely associated with Neoptolemos and Odysseus from the beginning of the play. They are the subjects of their king, as Neoptolemos is for some part of the play subject to Odysseus and the mission on which they were sent by the Greek army. In their first words (148–90/135–90), the chorus ask for instructions from Neoptolemos. The subservience of the chorus abolishes the distance between the actor on stage and the chorus in the orchestra. Their invocation of the scepter of Zeus that their "master," the boy Neoptolemos, possesses introduces the first of the three sacred objects that figure as bearers of power and authority in the play: the other objects are the arms of Achilles, fashioned by the god Hephaistos on Olympos, and the bow and arrows given to Philoctetes by Herakles on the summit of Mt. Oita. Only these appear on stage. The *skeptron* Agamemnon takes up in the assembly of the Greek army at the beginning of the *Iliad* is a hereditary possession fashioned by Hephaistos and passed down from Zeus to Agamemnon (2.100–6). The *skeptron* Achilles takes up in the assembly is seen very differently. Just as it will never sprout leaves again once cut from a tree, Achilles' oath never to return to battle for the Achaians is immutable (*Iliad* 1.234–44). Neoptolemos' men respect the traditional symbol of their king's authority.

The first reflections of the chorus turn to Philoctetes, who has not yet appeared from the lower opening of the cave. They can hear but they cannot see his agony and desolation (201/203). They enter into a dialogue with Neoptolemos and, as he appears, they address Philoctetes (313/317). In a formal ode, whose strophe is separated from its anti-strophe by more than the 100 lines in which Odysseus rehearses his plot, the chorus invoke the Earth, Mother of the Gods. In the strophe, they represent to Philoctetes the fictive scene on the Troad in which they and their injured king witnessed the award of the arms of Achilles to Odysseus. By their complicity in Odysseus' plot, they succeed in catching Philoctetes in its toils. They enlist Philoctetes in a community of loathing for Odysseus and the Greek army. In the long-delayed anti-strophe, they express once again their pity for Philoctetes' life on Lemnos.

In the only formal *stasimon*[16] of the play (696–751/676–728), the chorus return to the theme of Philoctetes' sufferings, once again in his presence. They can discover no parallel in history for his sufferings and find him innocent of any offense against god or man. The far-fetched example of Ixion, who was punished by Zeus by being bound to an eternally rotating wheel, is no precedent for Philoctetes' sufferings. The chorus conclude by endorsing Neoptolemos' promise to take him home. The depth of their involvement in Odysseus' plot to trick the object of their professed sympathy is evident as Philoctetes falls asleep, exhausted by the pain of his wound. The chorus sings a lyric invocation

---

16. That is, a formal song accompanied by dance and divided into *strophe* (turn) and *antistrophe* (counter-turn) when the chorus of fifteen have taken their position in the orchestra (after the *parados*, or entry song). In form, the other choral songs of the play are *kommoi*, or antiphonal lyrics (originally laments). These are 873–913/827–64 in which Neoptolemos responds to the chorus and 1200–1334/1081–1217 in which the chorus respond to Philoctetes.

to Sleep (Hypnos), the healer of mortal suffering. It is at this crucial moment that Neoptolemos resists their urging to leave with the bow entrusted to him and abandon Philoctetes on the island.

This moment is the pivot on which the play turns. Philoctetes awakes and Neoptolemos revolts from his long subordination to Odysseus and turns to Philoctetes whom he has now acquired "as a friend" (690/671). The chorus had reminded him of the favorable wind that had sprung up; Neoptolemos resists this wind. This wind has as much power over him now that he has received the bow of Herakles as has Odysseus' persuasive eloquence at the beginning of the play. Odysseus' plot would require him to abandon his inborn character "for a brief, shameless part of the day" (94/83). After the "sacrament of the bow," Neoptolemos is incapable of this.

In a striking way, it is Philoctetes and not the chorus who sustains the choral lyric for the rest of the play. His language is lyrical (in terms of both diction and meter) as he imagines what his life on Lemnos would be without his bow (1200–1344/1081–1222). Formally this final song is a dirge of lamentation (kommos) in which Philoctetes laments his fate as once again he is abandoned on Lemnos but now without his bow. The chorus respond in short perfunctory comments about Philoctetes being responsible for the destiny he is lamenting and exonerate themselves and Odysseus of any treachery. It is only at the end of the second antistrophe that Philoctetes pays any attention to what the chorus say and only because they have finally commented on his suffering (1287/1170). The worlds of the subordinate chorus and the wounded Philoctetes stand far apart. The chorus justify Odysseus' plot by claiming that he was aiding "friends" (1261/1145). The Greeks at Troy are not Philoctetes' "friends." For the chorus, Philoctetes and his bow are the means to preserving the "community" of the Greek army at Troy; for Philoctetes, his bow is the only means of sustaining his life on Lemnos. The decision of Neoptolemos to return the bow to the man he has acquired as a friend incorporates Philoctetes into another world of friendship.

Philoctetes is not entirely wrapped up in himself and the grim thought of his life on Lemnos without his bow. Unlike the island he says farewell to as he leaves for Troy, the Lemnos of these lyrics is not uninhabited. In the second strophe he imagines Odysseus seated on its shore gloating over the arms of Herakles (1236–53/1123–39). (Actually, Odysseus never gains possession of his bow.) In this song, the other inhabitants of Lemnos are the birds and game his bow (which he calls "my means of living" in 1239/1126) brings down. In his final farewell to the island and in the presence of Herakles and his bow (1647–71/1452–

68), Lemnos becomes what Homer called it, a "sacred island" (*Iliad* 21.79). It is haunted by nymphs of the meadows, Hermes, and Apollo of the Lycian spring. The chorus finally recognize the divinity of the place; they pray to the sea-nymphs as they sail to Troy. The homecoming they pray for will be delayed by the short episode of savagery that follows the capture of Troy.

The Bow

τῶι οὖν τόξωι ὄνομα βίος, ἔργον δὲ θάνατος

Life is the name of the bow; its work death.

—Herakleitos fr. 48 Diels-Kranz, *Die Fragmente der Vorsokratiker*

The bow of Philoctetes once belonged to Herakles, who gave it to his companion on Oita in thanks for lighting the pyre that consumed his body, freed him from pain, and rendered him immortal. He had employed it in the first Greek expedition against the Troy of Laomedon. Herakles the archer is impressively shown kneeling on one knee with the bow bent on the East pediment of the temple of Aphaia on Aegina (c. 500–480 B.C.). In Sophocles' *Philoctetes* the bow is both a prop to support Philoctetes as he limps on stage from his cave in the middle of the play and an object of awe. We do not see it at first. It is only when Philoctetes brings his bow from his cave as he prepares to leave for Skyros and Malis that it makes its long-delayed epiphany on stage. The young Neoptolemos stands in awe of it and asks if he can touch it and worship it, "as I would a god" (673/657). In first allowing Neoptolemos to hold his bow and then in entrusting it to him, Philoctetes reenacts the scene on Mt. Oita when Herakles entrusted the bow to him. As they enter the cave to gather Philoctetes' few possessions, Neoptolemos both holds Philoctetes' bow and supports Philoctetes himself. Philoctetes gives Neoptolemos his bow as he faints from the recurrent pain of his infection (790–93/762–66), and it remains in Neoptolemos' possession until he finally realizes that he cannot take leave of "his very nature" (956/902–3). After an outraged Odysseus has left the stage in frustration, Neoptolemos returns the bow to its rightful owner (1437/1286–87). Neoptolemos has discovered that the bow and its owner are inseparable.

As the two new comrades prepare to leave the island, the younger man supports the older, who carries his bow. Philoctetes tries to assure Neoptolemos that he will protect him against any reprisals by the Greek army with the arrows of Herakles (1593/1406). As he mentions the name Herakles, Herakles appears on the rock platform at the base of the upper cave.

The prospect of the two comrades facing insuperable odds is strangely reminiscent. In book 21 of the *Odyssey*, Odysseus and his son Telemachos face the suitors. Odysseus is armed with a bow given to him by Iphitos, who was murdered by Herakles (*Odyssey* 21.11–33). In a test of strength, Odysseus strings this great horn bow, drives an arrow through twelve ax heads, and with the help of Telemachos begins the slaughter of the suitors in his palace (*Odyssey* 21.258–22.125).

The tension between Philoctetes and Odysseus is not something that can be unstrung and relaxed like a bow or lyre. It is only Herakles who can resolve this tension and determine the destruction of the city he had attacked with Philoctetes a generation earlier. He has a divine influence on a man to whom he had given his bow and who has come to resemble him in his suffering. The snake that struck Philoctetes' foot has the same effect on him as the shirt of the centaur Nessos that consumed Herakles' body with its poison. The epiphany of Herakles as a deus ex machina is carefully prepared for. The appearance of his bow brings his divine power to mind. In his agony, Philoctetes had directed the attention of Neoptolemos and the audience upward to the ledge Herakles will stand on at the end of the play (854–58/814–16):

PHILOCTETES There now—over there—

NEOPTOLEMOS What are you saying? Where?

PHILOCTETES Up—

NEOPTOLEMOS What—Are you turning delirious again?
Why are you looking up at the sky?

The cue that brings Herakles on stage are Philoctetes' words "the arrows of Herakles" (1593/1406). There is little to prepare for this Euripidean resolution to human conflict in the tragedies of Sophocles. The striking precedent was Sophocles' *Athamas*, a lost play on the career of Athamas, his divine wife, Nephele, and his human wife, Ino. From indirect evidence we know that the threat to Athamas' life as a sacrificial victim was averted by the appearance of Herakles.[17]

The device of resolving a human impasse by the appearance of a god is familiar from the theater of Euripides. The *Hippolytus* opens with a prologue spoken by Aphrodite, a goddess offended by Hippoly-

17. See Sir Hugh Lloyd-Jones, *Sophocles* III: *Fragments* for what little is known of Sophocles' two Athamas plays.

tus' exclusive devotion to the virgin Artemis, and ends with the appearance of Artemis on the roof of Theseus' palace in Troizen. As Hippolytus lies maimed and at the point of death below her, she tidies up the human tragedy of Hippolytus, Phaedra, and Theseus by offering the consolation of the cult of the dying Hippolytus will receive in death. Perhaps the closest parallel in Euripides to the last scene of Sophocles' *Philoctetes* is from another lost play of Euripides, the *Antiope*. By our good luck, we know from a papyrus the shape of Euripides' "solution" to the conflict of this play. The two sons of Antiope and Zeus, Zethos and Amphion, are locked in a contest over their two very different ways of life: the political and the musical. The human conflict between the twin brothers has no solution, just as the struggle between Odysseus and Philoctetes over two forms of heroism can have no resolution. In the *Antiope*, it is only the appearance of Hermes at the end of the play that resolves the tension of the sons of Zeus and assures the building of the walls of Thebes.

The appearance of Herakles in Sophocles' *Philoctetes* assures the destruction of the walls of a city built by Apollo and Poseidon. The future seems honorable and prosperous for both Philoctetes and Neoptolemos who will combine to destroy the city of Priam. But Herakles' words to the two warriors headed for Troy are ominous (1633–34/1440–41):

> But remember, when you conquer the land,
> to respect what is sacred to the gods.

Anyone present in the theater of Dionysos in the spring contests of 409 understood how the young Neoptolemos became the bloodthirsty Pyrrhos once he reached Troy. Pyrrhos is slaughtered at Delphi, the shrine of Apollo; Philoctetes finally returns safely to his home to Malis (*Odyssey* 3.190).

Durham, North Carolina   DISKIN CLAY
February 2003

I wish to thank Sir Hugh Lloyd-Jones for the gift and guidance of the three volumes of his edition of Sophocles for the Loeb Classical Texts; Stephen Esposito for providing me a copy of William Arrowsmith's unpublished lecture on "The Sacrament of the Bow"; William Arrowsmith for his inspiration as a translator of dramatic texts; and, finally, Andrea Purvis, who in March 2000 helped me guide my colleague Carl Phillips.

ON THE TRANSLATION

It's proverbial, of course, that something gets lost in translation. What gets lost is an entire sensibility unique to—and enacted by—the original, and what too often gets compromised is a parallel uniqueness contained by—and enacted by—the language into which the original has been translated.

Rather than try to replicate in English certain strengths of the Greek original, I have tried to replicate the *effect* of those strengths by determining and then employing the particular strengths of English, with attention to how those strengths contribute to free verse especially. I had no interest in trying to force the accentual-syllabic English into the quantitative jacket of Greek, or in seeking to match up the Greek line with, say, the English blank verse line, as if the two were the same or even close.

The most immediately obvious aspect of my translation will be the frequent and radical shifts in line length throughout. In part, I felt this would be a means of conveying the constant shifts in morality, in the notion of trust, and in emotional temper in the course of the play. I want the lines to reflect, as well, the wildness of the landscape in which they occur, and the ruggedness—the harshness and brutality—that characterized the military life in the Homeric age during which this play takes place. The risk here is one of randomness and self-indulgence; to these, I can only counter with an assurance to my readers that, in the course of many years of reading the play in the original and in the many translations that have appeared and continue to appear, I have worked hard to hear the nuances—emotional, psychological, and in terms of language—that resonate through the Philoctetes legend as Sophocles himself wanted it to be told; and I have then gauged my lines accordingly.

I intend for there to be an audible pause at the end of each line, a sharp stress at each line's beginning—the silences are just as important as the spoken parts, and a vocal hesitation is not unrelated to a hesitation of psyche. In a play of so little physical action, relatively speaking, what is clear in the Greek—and crucial to bring to the fore in the English—is that there *is* action, and a great deal of it; but in this play more than any of the other extant tragedies, the action is almost entirely intellectual, psychological, and of the gut. The Greek registers these shifts via metrical shift—there is, if not a metrical equivalent for each state of being human, then a capacity for the Greek to accommodate the nuances of those states with the meter. To read Greek is to know sonically the difference between sudden grief and frenzy, between bliss hoped for and bliss received. My hope is that these shifts might be recognizable, here, in the shifting of line length and in the ways in which the possibilities of line length and line break get deployed on the page.

In addition to line length and line break, syntax and the manipulation of it have been essential tools for me in drawing forth the nuances of (to give but one example) the stalling that is sometimes crisis, sometimes wonder, other times a moment of internal resolve on the part of one character or another. I wish to emphasize that I am in no way seeking to imitate the inflected quality of ancient Greek; rather, the intention here is to take fullest advantage of the capacity for syntax to reflect and enact psychology and emotion, and to make the reader (and listener) an active participant in such psychology or emotion. The result is, necessarily, not entirely demotic, but this has not seemed inappropriate, finally, for a play in which neither the characters nor the moral dilemmas they play out are ever without seriousness and rigor. And again, so much of the action of the play occurs at the level of "ordinary" conversational exchange: no word is without its valence here, and I have worked to calibrate the syntax so as to make these valences most clear.

Given the extraordinarily high number of exclamations of agony and pain in the play, I had to arrive at a means of conveying those moments without seeming redundant and ultimately risking an unwanted comic effect. Too many instances of "alas!" and "ah me," and melodrama, stirring, rears its head. After much debate, it seemed to me inaccurate to merely transliterate the Greek exclamations—they announced right away their being out of place, given that the point was to render an English translation; as well, such expressions are as untranscribable as gesture itself. To attempt that sort of transcription or transliteration seemed to me to have the effect that occurs when we convey pain and assault as "aargh" and "pow," respectively. Fine for the comics, but unsuited finally to the higher seriousness of tragedy. With the exception, therefore, of the occasional "alas" or "ah me"—which, after all, people *do* still say in English—I have chosen to replace such moments with a stage direction indicating the need (and freedom) for the actor to express pain as seems most authentic and appropriate—and for the reader, accordingly, to do the same on the level of imagination.

The lyrical moments in tragedy occur in the choruses. Here, though, *Philoctetes* proves to be a sometime exception. Ordinarily, to enter the choral passages is to step from the dramatic, narrative mode and into the more reflective, meditative, and more suspended or static mode we call the lyric. But it is easy to read this particular play in English and miss the lyric quality of many of the choruses, since they often consist of dialogue, conversational exchange between the soldiers and another character in the play, and are therefore indistinguishable, *in terms of content*, from the narrative body of the play. Consider, for example, such passages as 148–214 and 1200–87, both of them instances in which the chorus has a dialogue with, respectively, Neoptolemus and Philoctetes—or, more accurate, the lyric chorus is variously interrupted or complemented by the recitative dialogue of the other character. In the Greek, the choruses are immediately distinguishable by their lyric meters and their strophic patterning. I have adhered to my choice of flexible line length in the choruses, but have coupled that with a tempered regularity—that is, the stanzas themselves are heterometric, but matched (within a single chorus) in terms of the number of lines per strophic movement—so as to bring forward, visually at least, the patterns of strophe and antistrophe that especially distinguish the choruses from the text around them.

What I have most hoped to bring out in my translation is the complexity of the intimacy with which this play is at every point charged. There is an intimacy born of isolation—consider the intimacy that marks the relationship between Philoctetes and the island (and its animal inhabitants); that to which he was once abandoned has become all he knows and therefore clings to. A parallel intimacy exists between Philoctetes and the all-but-anthropomorphized bow—not to mention the intimacy between arrow and bow: an intimacy so heightened, that each is useless without the other. To this extent, we might call the relationship between bow and arrow a symbiotic one—and quickly see it as a paradigm for one aspect of the relationship between Philoctetes and Neoptolemos.

Another aspect of that relationship is filial-once-removed, as it were: Neoptolemos is a man without a father—has never, in fact, seen his father alive—and quickly adopts a filial relationship to his father's comrade-in-arms, Philoctetes. Part of the recognition and acceptance of this relationship is indicated by how often Philoctetes refers to Neoptolemos as "teknon"—child, or son—a form of address that not only reinforces the father-son relationship, but is resonant as well with the multiplicity of things that Philoctetes is to Neoptolemos: a superior officer as well as a father figure; an elder, and at the same time a man whose chance for heroism depends entirely on the younger man who is his subordinate.

Fraternity is another important component—and form of intimacy—in this play. Philoctetes is the only all-male tragedy that survives; and not only is the cast made up entirely of men, but of soldiers, who are joined together and dependent on one another even more than the average group of men; after all, the success of military action depends on working in concert. In the line of battle, each man becomes as much protector as the object of protection—the difference it could make was that between life and death. Again, bow and arrow. Somewhere in here, it is not only possible to see an erotic aspect of intimacy at work—it is necessary, I believe, to do so. By this, I mean the way in which it is impossible to remove entirely the erotic—the homoerotic—from the fraternal. There is a difference between the sexual and the erotic—it is of the latter that I speak here.

It is my sense that the absolute maleness of the cast has everything to do with the increasing claustrophobia—psychologically—of this play. What is claustrophobia, finally, but intimacy at too intense a pitch—intimacy as much with place as with people, in this case. And an intimacy with ideas or conventions—specifically, trust and duty, on which so many of the intimacies in the play crucially and perilously depend. Again, it is through line length and syntactical inflection that I have hoped to convey the intricacies of intimacy—itself ever shifting—across the play.

This translation is of the Greek in the Oxford Classical text of A. C. Pearson, as reprinted in Webster's edition of the play (*Sophocles: Philoctetes*, T.B.L. Webster, ed., Cambridge University Press, Cambridge, 1997). With regard to method, I translated the play flat out, as it were—leaving no word untranslated, nothing elided in terms of content—in a single week. Then began the process of lineation, which, as in my own poems, got determined after many readings of the text aloud. Several mail exchanges took place between myself and Diskin Clay, whom I thank for pointing out to me the occasional awkwardness or possible misstep, and for his enthusiastic support of and belief in the necessary strangenesses I have brought to the translation of this play, with the hope that *Philoctetes* might be understood as Sophocles himself wanted his audience to understand it.

St. Louis, Missouri   CARL PHILLIPS
February 2003

PHILOCTETES

CHARACTERS

ODYSSEUS son of Laertes

NEOPTOLEMOS son of Achilles

PHILOCTETES son of Poias of Malis

CHORUS a contingent of sailors, who have arrived on Lemnos with Neoptolemos from the island of Skyros.

TRADER actually Odysseus in disguise

HERAKLES

Nonspeaking parts The men of Odysseus who enter at 1061
One of Neoptolemos' men, who accompanies Neoptolemos and Odysseus from the opening of the play until 147.

The scene is a cliff on the coast of the island of Lemnos. Overlooking the sea, there is a cave with two entrances, one above the other. Some rags draped on the rocks to dry are the only signs of human presence.

ODYSSEUS *enters the stage platform, followed by* NEOPTOLEMOS *and the sailor who does not speak.* ODYSSEUS *gestures to the rock cliff above and addresses* NEOPTOLEMOS, *who stands nearer to the stage building. The orchestra represents the shore of Lemnos. The* CHORUS *begin to assemble in the orchestra after* ODYSSEUS BEGINS TO SPEAK.

ODYSSEUS This coast—

This shore—

This is Lemnos, the sea
surrounds it. No man
lives here—even
steps here.

Neoptolemos, son of Achilles—himself, of all the
      Greeks, the noblest father—
it's in this place that, at the command of those in
      charge, I left
the Malian, the son of Poias, his foot
all but consumed by   10
the disease with which it festered—
                      Always,
no sooner would we attend to the usual libations
      or sacrifices,
he'd fill our whole camp with his wild and far-from-
      good-omened
cries—
      Groaning: howling:

Why speak of it now?

33

This is hardly the hour for long speeches—
he may find out I'm here,
I may give away the very plan by which   20
I intend to snare him, soon enough.

Your job: help me with the details—specifically,
look for where these rocks become a double-mouthed
  cave—
forming in winter a sort of twin sun-seat,
while in summer a breeze can send sleep through the
  cave at both ends . . .
Below it, to the left, you should see
a small spring of drinking water—if it's still there,
  that is.
Go ahead,
quietly,
signal whether he's still in the same place,
  or elsewhere,   30
then I'll tell you the rest of the story,
and you can hear it—our goal's
the same one.

NEOPTOLEMOS Odysseus—Sir—what you speak of, it
    isn't far. At least I think I can see the cave you've
    mentioned.

ODYSSEUS Above? or below?

NEOPTOLEMOS Above. No sound of footsteps.

ODYSSEUS Make sure he's not camped out asleep.

NEOPTOLEMOS I see a sort of house, but it's empty—nobody there.

ODYSSEUS No sign of anyone living in it?   40

NEOPTOLEMOS Some ground cover, crushed, as if from someone
    lying on it.

ODYSSEUS But the rest is deserted? Nothing beneath the roof?

> NEOPTOLEMOS *enters the cave above the stage platform*
> *and looks about.*

NEOPTOLEMOS A wooden cup—the work of an amateur—along with
some firewood.

ODYSSEUS They must be his—his stores, such as they are.

NEOPTOLEMOS —And these too: some rags drying out, pus-heavy . . .

ODYSSEUS Well, it's clear that he lives here, and isn't
too far away. How far could he go,
with his foot diseased all this time?
He's gone to look for food, maybe,
he may know of some herb that eases the pain.   50
Send the man you have with you as a scout, so that
          no one catches me—
of all the Argives, there's none he'd rather take than
          me.

> *The silent sailor moves away to stand guard on stage*
> *near the entrance of the cave.*

NEOPTOLEMOS He's going—consider the path guarded.—If you
          need anything,
say so.

ODYSSEUS Son of Achilles,
for the business you're involved in,
you'll have to be as noble as your birth is—
not only in body, but also, should you learn of
          something you haven't
heard of before, you must help me.
You are, after all, my assistant—   60

NEOPTOLEMOS What is your command?

ODYSSEUS With your words,
capture the mind—the very soul—of Philoctetes.

When he asks you who you are, where you're from,
    say:
"I am the son of Achilles." This needn't be kept
    secret.

And—

And you are sailing home, you've abandoned
    the Achaian fleet,
full of hate for those who first entreated you with
    prayers to leave home,
saying that you were their only hope of sacking Troy—
and then they didn't give you the arms of Achilles
    when you came and,   70
quite rightly, asked for them.
No—instead, they gave them to Odysseus.
Say whatever you wish about me—the most
    abominable things you can think of,
it won't bother me. If you
don't do this, you bring grief to all the Argives:
for if this man's bow isn't captured, you'll have no
    chance at all of taking Troy.

As to how it is that any dealing with this man can be
    trustworthy and safe
for you, and not at all for me—Listen:
You sailed under oath to no one,
nor out of necessity,   80
nor as part of the first expedition—
I can't say the same for myself, however, on any of
    these counts.
Therefore, if, while still in possession of his bow, he
    should see me,
—I am dead, and you
with me, as my accomplice.

This is what we must devise,
you to be the one to rob him of his invincible arms.
I know you aren't, by nature, the sort to lie,
or to plot evil, but

—isn't it sweet to gain victory?—   90

dare to. Let us be honest
at another time;
for now,
for a brief, shameless part of the day, give me
yourself—
and ever after, be known as the most honorable
        of men.

NEOPTOLEMOS Son of Laertes, I hate doing things that are painful
        even to listen to.
I wasn't born to act by deception,
nor, so they say, was my father before me.
I'm willing to take the man by force,   100
not by trickery—he can hardly take *us* by force, on a
        single leg.

Though sent as your helper, I refuse to be called
        a traitor.
I'd rather fail while acting nobly, than win dishonestly
any victory.

ODYSSEUS You're the son of a noble father.
I myself, when I was younger, had an idle tongue,
and a working hand.
But now that it comes to the test,
I see that it's the tongue, and not deeds,
that commands all things for mortals.   110

NEOPTOLEMOS But what do you order me to say, if not lies?

ODYSSEUS I'm telling you to seize Philoctetes by trickery.

NEOPTOLEMOS But why by trickery? Why not,
            instead, persuasion?

ODYSSEUS He isn't persuadable, and you won't likely take him
         by force.

NEOPTOLEMOS What makes him so sure of his strength?

ODYSSEUS His arrows—as inescapable as is the death they bring
         with them.

NEOPTOLEMOS And it's not safe even to approach him?

ODYSSEUS Not unless you take him by trickery, as I've said.

NEOPTOLEMOS Don't you think it's shameful to tell lies?   120

ODYSSEUS No—not if lying is a means to safety.

NEOPTOLEMOS How can you look me in the eye and say such
            things aloud?

ODYSSEUS When to act means to gain an advantage, there's no
         need for scruples.

NEOPTOLEMOS What advantage is there for *me* in his coming to Troy?

ODYSSEUS Only this bow of his will take Troy.

NEOPTOLEMOS Then I'm not the one who will take the city,
            as you said?

ODYSSEUS Neither you without the bow, nor the bow
         without you.

NEOPTOLEMOS In that case, it must be captured.

ODYSSEUS Especially since, in doing this, you'll take away
         two prizes.

NEOPTOLEMOS What are they? I'd be quicker to act, if I knew.   130

ODYSSEUS To be called wise. To be called brave.

NEOPTOLEMOS Fine then. I'll do it, and
        put all shame aside.

ODYSSEUS Then you remember what I told you to do?

NEOPTOLEMOS Yes, I've agreed to it, haven't I?

ODYSSEUS You stay and wait for him here—I'm off,
                            CHORUS *enters.*
        so he won't catch sight of me.
        I'll send the scout back to the ship,
        but if you seem to be taking too long,
        I'll send the same man back, but disguised,
           as a captain—   140
        that way, he won't be recognized.
        He's a spinner of tales, that one—
        Take only what seems most useful in what he says.
        I'm going to the ship now—I leave the rest to you.
        May Hermes the cunning leader be
        our leader, along with Victory,
        and Athena too—she has always protected me.
                    Exit ODYSSEUS *and sailor.*

CHORUS What is it,   *strophe*
        what must I hide, my lord—
        I, a stranger in this, a strange land—   130
        or what say to a man so suspicious?
        Tell me.
        For his cunning surpasses that of others,
        as does the wisdom of kings—those who wield the
           divine scepter of Zeus.
        All this ancient mastery has come to you, young man—
        tell me, then: what must I do to help you?

NEOPTOLEMOS For now—since perhaps you'd like to look at
                     the place
             where he lies—look with confidence.
             But when the terrible wanderer comes from his
                     quarters,
             keep an eye out for my hand-signal,   160
             and try to help as seems best.

CHORUS   The care you speak of has long been our own,
                     my lord—   *antistrophe*
             to keep watch over your best interests.
             But where does he live, what house?
             That much, at least, I need to know,
             to be on guard for
             —and avoid—being
             ambushed by him.
             Where is he now—
             at home? outdoors somewhere?   170

NEOPTOLEMOS Well, you can see his house here, with the double
                     openings—a rocky resting-place—

CHORUS   And the victim himself?

NEOPTOLEMOS It's clear to me that it's out of hunger he makes his
                     labored way
             somewhere. For this is the sort of life he is said
                     to lead—
             in pain,
             painfully hunting with his winged arrows, no man
             approaching him with any respite from
             his sufferings.

CHORUS   I pity the man. No one cares for him,   *strophe*
             he has no one to look to. Wretched. Alone, always.   180
             he suffers this terrible disease—with each need as it
                     comes, he's
             lost again. How does he keep going?
             Strategems of the gods—unlucky race of man,

to whom there is no fair measure in this life.

This man may well be no inferior in birth to the
        best-born,   *antistrophe*
yet he lies alone, apart from all others,
except the spotted and hairy beasts—pitiable
in his hunger, in his sufferings, his miseries
        without cure.
And babbling Echo, appearing in the distance, merely
throws back to him his pitiable complaints.   190

NEOPTOLEMOS None of this surprises me.
        For, as I understand it, these sufferings are the will of
            the gods,
        and came upon him from savage-minded Chryse,
        and the things that he now endures, companionless,
        these too must be the design of the gods,
        so that he cannot send his invincible weapons
            against Troy
        until the time when it is determined that Troy must
            be destroyed
        by those weapons.

CHORUS Silence!—

NEOPTOLEMOS What is it?   200

CHORUS I heard a sound—as of someone in great
            pain—   *strophe*
        here, or—or over there.
        It's coming to me, yes: the voice of one who makes
            his way in agony—
        from afar, a man suffering—heavy groans—
        his lament coming clearly.
        You should take—

NEOPTOLEMOS What? Tell me.

CHORUS A new plan of action,   *antistrophe*
        since he isn't far off, but somewhere inside—   210

and he's not playing flute-songs, like some meadowing
    shepherd, but
either stumbling somewhere and in hardship
he lets go a far-reaching howl, or perhaps
he has seen the ship-grudging harbor.

    PHILOCTETES *has barely emerged from the entrance to*
his cave closest to the stage; he hesitates as he listens to
    NEOPTOLEMOS *speak to his men, then limps toward*
                         the group.

PHILOCTETES Strangers—
who are you, who have oared your way here,
a desolation
no better to drop anchor at than to live in?
What nationality, what race might I say is yours?
Your attire is that of Greece, the country most beloved
    by me.
Let me hear a voice—do not fear me and   220
panic at my wildness, no; but
pitying a man so ill-starred and alone and suffering as
    I am, and with
no friend, no companion—please, speak—if you have
    in fact come as friends—
Do answer—
for it isn't right that we should not have at least this
    much from each other.

NEOPTOLEMOS Stranger, since you wish to know it—
this much first: we are Greeks.

PHILOCTETES O most welcome voice—To be addressed by such a
    man, a Greek,
after all this time!
Child, what need brought you here and caused you
    to disembark?   230
What impulse?
Which, of all the winds, the most favoring?
Tell me everything, that I might learn who you are.

NEOPTOLEMOS I am from the island of Skyros.
I sail for home.
I am called Neoptolemos, son of Achilles.
And now you know everything.

PHILOCTETES Son of a dearest father, of a dear country,
nursling of old Lykomedes,
on what mission have you come here — and where are
you sailing   240
from?

NEOPTOLEMOS At the moment, I sail from Troy.

PHILOCTETES What do you mean? For you certainly weren't a
shipmate of
ours at the beginning of the expedition to Troy —

NEOPTOLEMOS Were you also a part of that effort?

PHILOCTETES Child, don't you know me, even looking at me?

NEOPTOLEMOS How should I know someone I've never seen before?

PHILOCTETES So you don't know my name, or anything of the
sufferings with which
I am utterly destroyed?

NEOPTOLEMOS No — nothing.   250

PHILOCTETES How wretched I am,
how hated by the gods,
if no word of my plight has reached home or, for
that matter,
any part of Greece at all.
Those who abandoned me here, against all that is
holy, they
mock me in silence,
while my disease continues and only grows worse.

43

Child—son of Achilles—
I am he whom perhaps you've heard of,
the master of the arms of Herakles, the son of Poias—   260
I am Philoctetes,
whom the two generals, along with Odysseus,
disgracefully left behind in this wilderness—

I'd been stricken with a grievous disease,
after being bitten by a venomous serpent.
On top of this,
having put in here with their fleet en route from
        sea-ringed Chryse,
they left me here—me, and my sickness.
Then, as—how gladly!—they saw me,
exhausted from so much tossing at sea,   270
sleeping in a rocky cave along the shore—
then, they abandoned me, leaving some
worn rags, and a small supply of food—the stuff
of beggars. I hope *they* come to as much!
What sort of waking from sleep do you imagine
        it was, child,
when they'd gone?
Of what sort, the evils I lamented, shed tears for,
seeing the very ships that I'd set out on now
gone entirely, no man around, who might help me
        when worn by disease.
Looking at everything, I discovered nothing was here
        except   280
suffering—of this, there was a great abundance.

Time, as it does, passing,
I made do for myself under this makeshift roof.
This bow, felling doves in flight, found what food
        I needed,
and whatever the arrow, drawn back in its string,
        brought down for me
—alone, abject, I crawled up to it,
dragging my miserable foot behind me.

If I needed drinking water in winter, when all water
     had turned ice,
still I managed, though suffering, to break up some
     wood.
Even then, no fire forthcoming—but by rubbing stone   290
against stones, I soon made the hidden flame appear,
which always rescued me.
For this roof, along with fire, provides me everything
except some respite from disease.

Come, child—now you need to learn about the island
     itself.
No sailor travels to it willingly.
For there's no harbor, really, nor anywhere that one
     might sail to
for conducting trade or enjoying any hospitality.
This is no destination for men of any sense.
Perhaps someone unwillingly comes here—for
     many things   300
can happen in the course of a man's life—
these people, when they *do* come, feel sorry for me,
at least according to their words,
and they've even given me a bit of food, or some
     clothing,
out of pity.
But this one thing, when I mention it, none is willing
     to do:
namely, to bring me home to safety.
Therefore, I am wasting away—for ten years now,
in hunger and in suffering,
feeding the disease whose hunger is endless.   310
Such things the Atreidai and violent Odysseus did
     to me—
may the Olympian gods give to them in return what I
     have suffered.

CHORUS Like the strangers who have come here before,
        I too pity you, son of Poias.

45

NEOPTOLEMOS   And I myself am witness to your words, that they
      are true—
     I know this, having also found the Atreidai and fierce
      Odysseus to be evil men.

PHILOCTETES   What complaint do you have with the ruinous
      Atreidai,
     what suffering is behind *your* anger?

NEOPTOLEMOS   May I satisfy someday my anger by this hand of mine,
     so that the Myceneans will know—and Sparta too— 320
     that Skyros is also the mother of brave men.

PHILOCTETES   You've spoken well. But tell me—what is it, that
     makes you come accusing them so angrily?

NEOPTOLEMOS   Son of Poias, though it's with difficulty that I tell you,
     I shall tell you
     the things I suffered at their hands, on
     reaching Troy.
     For when the fated time came for Achilles to die—

PHILOCTETES   Ah, no—Say nothing more, until I learn of this first:
     the son of Peleus is dead? 330

NEOPTOLEMOS   He is dead—shot by no man, but by a god, they say—
     struck down by Apollo.

PHILOCTETES   Then both of them—the slain and the one who slew
      him—are noble indeed.
     But I don't know whether I should first inquire into
      your suffering,
     or should grieve for this man.

NEOPTOLEMOS   I believe your own griefs are enough for you—
     poor soul—
     no need to grieve for the sufferings of anyone else.

PHILOCTETES I suppose you are right—

Tell me, then, of your situation, how they
    insulted you.   340

NEOPTOLEMOS On a garlanded ship,
    they came for me—
    godlike Odysseus, and Phoinix, the man who had
        reared my father.
    They said—the truth,
    or not, who knows?—that it was not the gods' will,
    now that my father had died,
    for anyone but myself to take Troy's citadel. And
        saying this,
    they did not need to spend much time urging me
    to sail soon—especially given my longing for the
        dead man,
    my wanting to see him while still unburied;   350
    for I had not seen him, ever.
    Moreover, there was the good news that if I went
        to Troy,
    I would capture it.
    I had sailed two days, when by oar and the wind's
        favor
    I reached hateful Sigeion.
    And immediately, the entire army, once I'd
        disembarked,
    surrounded me,
    swearing they saw Achilles again, though he was dead.

    —For he did lie dead.

    And I, wretched—when I'd wept for him,   360
    soon approached the Atreidai—my friends, or so
        it seemed—
    and requested my father's weapons and whatever other
        effects there might be.
    Alas—

they told me the worst thing possible:
"Son of Achilles, you can certainly have anything else,
but another man is lord of those arms now—the son
        of Laertes."

I burst into tears, and fell into a heavy rage, and said
        in grief:
"You monsters—you have dared to give to someone
        other than me
the arms that by rights are my own, before informing
        me?"

And Odysseus said—for he happened to be standing
        there—   370
"Yes, they gave them to me,
and rightly so.
I was there,
I am the one who saved the weapons and the corpse
        of Achilles."

I was infuriated, and insulted him in every way,
leaving nothing out, since he was going to rob me of
        the arms that were mine.

When it had come to this point,
and even though he wasn't prone to anger,
he was stung by what he'd heard, and answered
        me thus:
"You weren't where we were; no,   380
you were off where you shouldn't have been.
And now that you have spoken so insolently, you will
        never sail to Skyros
in possession of these arms, or anything else."

Hearing myself reproached with these terrible words,
I sailed for home, deprived of what is mine, by that
        worst of all evil men,
Odysseus.
Not that I blame *him* so much as I do

those in power; for the entire city, the whole army
is in the hands of those who rule; those men who are
      wanting
in discipline become evil by the example of their
      teachers.   390

That is the whole story.
And he who hates the Atreidai,
may he be a friend both to me and to the gods alike.

CHORUS Mountainous, all-grazing Earth—   *strophe*
      mother of Zeus himself, you
      who dwell in great Paktolos, rich in gold—

      when the arrogance of the Atreidai came against him,
      when they gave to the son of Laertes this man's
          father's arms

      even then, holy mother, I called upon you,
      the blessed rider of bull-devouring lions,   400
      an object of wonder beyond all others.

PHILOCTETES Strangers, you've sailed here, it seems,
      bearing a mark of suffering not unfamiliar to me,
      for it fits what I know myself of the deeds of
          the Atreidai, and of Odysseus.
      For I have known him to put his tongue to any
          speech that is evil,
      any outrage, by which he might bring about an
          injustice.
      But what I *do* wonder is
      how the mighty Ajax can have endured seeing these
          things, if he was present.

NEOPTOLEMOS He was no longer alive—
      had he been, I'd never have been stripped of my arms.   410

PHILOCTETES What do you mean? Even he lives now among
      the dead?

NEOPTOLEMOS Put it this way: he no longer lives in the light.

PHILOCTETES Alas—but Diomedes,
and Odysseus, begot by Sisyphos and sold to Laertes—
they aren't dead, when they more rightly *should* be!

NEOPTOLEMOS Indeed—be assured of that—in fact, even now they
are thriving in the Argive army.

PHILOCTETES Alas . . .
And my old friend, noble Nestor, of Pylos,
is *he* alive?
For he'd have stopped their outrages, by his wise
counsel.   420

NEOPTOLEMOS Just now, he fares badly,
since Antilochos—his son—has died and left him.

PHILOCTETES Ah—you have spoken of two men,
whom I would least wish to have meet with death,
alas—
What is one to look toward, now that these men
are dead,
while Odysseus—whom
it would be more fitting to call dead—
is very much alive?

NEOPTOLEMOS A clever wrestler, that one.   430
But even cleverness gets often enough tripped up,
Philoctetes.

PHILOCTETES By the gods, tell me this:
where was Patroklos in all of this—he who was
everything to your father?

NEOPTOLEMOS Dead also. I shall teach you something in a very
few words:
war never chooses to take the disgraceful man,
but will always prefer those who are most noble.

PHILOCTETES I can attest to that. On this subject,
      let me ask you about one who is hardly noble, but is
         clever and wise
      where his tongue's concerned—how's *he* faring now?   440

NEOPTOLEMOS Whom do you mean, if not Odysseus?

PHILOCTETES Not him, but a certain Thersites, who was never
         content to speak
      just once, even when no one wished him to speak to
         begin with.
      Do you know if he's alive?

NEOPTOLEMOS I've not seen him myself, but I have heard he's
         living still.

PHILOCTETES How fitting! Nothing evil has ever died.
      On the contrary, the gods guard it well. Somehow,
      whatever is villainous and thoroughly wicked—this
         they bless,
      even keeping it from Hades.
      But what's just, what's noble,   450
      this they destroy always.
      How to account for this, how approve it,
      when in looking upon matters divine, I find the gods
      themselves are evil?

NEOPTOLEMOS I for one, from now on, shall look upon Troy and
         the Atreidai from
      a great distance,
      and I shall be on guard against them.
      When the worse man is stronger than the better man,
      and what's good is destroyed and what's wicked is
         in power,
      I shall not bear such men, not ever.   460

      No,
      from now on let rocky Skyros be enough for me,
      so that I can have some pleasure at home.

—But now I head for the ship. And you, son of Poias,
goodbye,
and farewell,
and may the gods relieve you of your sickness, as
        you wish.

                              To his companions.

—Let's go, so that whenever the god sees fit for us to
        sail, we may do so.

PHILOCTETES But—
are you going already?   470

NEOPTOLEMOS Yes—we must take advantage of the chance to set sail,
not when it calls from afar, but now,
while it's at hand.

PHILOCTETES By your father—by your mother—
child, if there is anything dear to you at home, by
that too, I beg you:
do not leave me here, alone, suffering such evils—
living among them—as you see, and have heard.
Don't think me a burden.
There's a lot of trouble, yes, to my being brought
        along with you,   480
but undertake it, all the same.
For, among noble men, the disgraceful deed is an
        object of hate, but
the noble one is well spoken of.
In refusing my request, you win for yourself
shame only;
but in doing it—child, if I return to Oita alive,
the greatest honor, that of good reputation, is yours.

Come—
it's an inconvenience of not even an entire day—
        dare it,
take me aboard, and put me in the hold,   490

52

on the prow, at the stern, wherever
I'll be the least burdensome to your crew.

Promise—
by suppliant Zeus himself,
child, be persuaded—I fall on my knees before you,
even as weak and suffering as I am, and so lame.
Don't leave me here to suffer as an outcast from the
    step of men,
no.
Either take me safe to your home, or to Chalkedon
    on Euboia.
From there, it's not much of a journey for me to the
    swift-flowing river of   500
Spercheios, so that you might show me to my dear
    father
—for a long time now I have feared he is no longer
    with us.
For I sent many messages to him by those who have
    chanced here,
many requests begging him to make the journey here
    himself and
deliver me safely home.—But he is either dead,
or the business of the messengers, likely enough,
outweighed my own, and they voyaged straight home.

But now—for in you I come across both a leader and
    a messenger—
save me,
have mercy on me,   510
since for better or worse, men must
endure what's terrible and
dangerous, both.
When free from distress, we should be on the alert for
    what's terrible,
and when life is going well, look especially
then to our lives,
that they haven't been destroyed while we weren't
    looking.

CHORUS Pity him, my lord.   *antistrophe*
He has made clear the struggles of many all-but-
        unbearable troubles,
such as may no friend of mine come to know.   520
If you hate the wicked Atreidai, lord,
I myself would make from their evil an advantage for
        this man,
and I would take him on our well-fitted, swift ship
to where he is eager to go—namely, home,
escape from the wrath of the gods.

NEOPTOLEMOS See that you don't now seem generous-minded,
and then appear a stranger to your own words, when
        you've had
your fill of contact with his disease.

CHORUS Far from it. you will never be able to accuse me of
        that, or not justly.

NEOPTOLEMOS It is disgraceful, though, for me to appear less
        willing than   530
yourselves to do what is proper. If it seems best,
        let us sail,
let's set out quickly.
For the ship won't refuse to carry him—
may the gods carry *us* from this land safely,
to wherever we wish to sail.

PHILOCTETES Dearest day, sweetest man, beloved sailors—
by what deed might I show you how full of love you
        have made me
toward yourselves?
Child, let us go—having given, though, due
        homage to
the inside of this house, not exactly a house—   540
that you might learn how I survived, how brave I was.
For I believe that, except for myself,
no one would have endured it, having looked inside.

But, by necessity, I learned to bear my hardships.
                              Begins to enter the cave.

CHORUS Stop—Stand still.
        Two men are coming, a captain from your ship, and a
            foreigner—
        find out about them first; then go in.

                    Enter Odysseus, disguised as a trader. He is
                    accompanied by another member of the crew who
                                        does not speak.

TRADER Son of Achilles—I asked this fellow, a trader like
            myself, who was standing
        guard with two others over your ship—I asked him to
            tell me where you were—
        seeing as I'd encountered your crew, not planning to,
            but   550
        just happening to drop anchor in the same spot.
        For as a sea captain I sail with a small crew from
            Ilion to
        grape-bearing Peparethos—home—
        When I heard that all these sailors were yours,
        I decided not to make my journey in silence, without
        speaking to you and finding some recompense.
        For you aren't completely aware of your own affairs—
        what new plots there are concerning you among
            the Argives,
        not just plots—no longer in-progress—
        no: in effect already.   560

NEOPTOLEMOS Stranger, if I am not an evil man,
            the courtesy of your forethought will remain as token
                of friendship.
            Tell me the deeds of which you've spoken,
            so I may know the latest plans against me among
                the Argives.

TRADER They have gone in pursuit of you—Phoinix, and the
            sons of Theseus—
    complete with a ship's crew.

NEOPTOLEMOS To bring me back by violence, or with words?

TRADER I don't know. I stand simply as messenger before you.

NEOPTOLEMOS And Phoinix and his shipmates, are they doing this
            willingly,
    as a favor to the Atreidai?   570

TRADER Be sure of this: these things are not the future—
    they are happening even now.

NEOPTOLEMOS But how is it that Odysseus is not prepared to sail
            here as his own messenger?
    Does some fear hold him back?

TRADER Odysseus and the son of Tydeus were off in search of
            somebody else,
    when I myself set out.

NEOPTOLEMOS Who was this man whom Odysseus sailed in
            search of?

TRADER He was a certain—
    but first, tell me who this man here is.
    And when speaking, don't speak too loudly.   580

NEOPTOLEMOS Stranger, this is the renowned Philoctetes, no doubt
            known to yourself.

TRADER Then don't ask me anything else.
    Sail as quickly as you can.
    Get off this island.

PHILOCTETES   *To* NEOPTOLEMOS.
    What is he saying, child?

What business is the sailor conducting with you
    in secret?

NEOPTOLEMOS I don't know quite what he's saying. But he ought to
    say what he has to say
in the open,
to you, me, and these men with us.

TRADER Son of Achilles: do not slander me before the army   590
for saying what I should not.
For, in doing many favors on their behalf, I enjoy
    many benefits in return,
though a poor man myself.

NEOPTOLEMOS I am hated by them.
This man is my dearest friend, for he hates
    the Atreidai.
If you have come to me as a friend,
you must hide from us nothing that you have heard.

TRADER Watch what you're doing, young man.

NEOPTOLEMOS I have long been careful, and am careful even now.

TRADER I shall lay all blame on you.   600

NEOPTOLEMOS Do so. Now speak.

TRADER Fine—I shall.
The two men you heard about—the son of Tydeus,
    and mighty Odysseus—
it is after this man here they're sailing,
bound by oath, either to bring him back by the
    persuasion of words,
or that of sheer force.
And all the Achaians heard Odysseus say this clearly:
he was more confident of getting this done than was
    his accomplice.

NEOPTOLEMOS But, after all this time, by what reasoning do
    the Atreidai concern themselves
  with a man whom, years ago, they cast out?   610
  What can they be longing for?
  Or is it the violence and anger with which the gods
    punish wickedness—
  have these brought them to this point?

TRADER I'll explain everything, since obviously you've
    not heard.
  There was a certain seer of noble birth—son of Priam—
    called Helenos,
  whom this man—Odysseus, who is called every
  foul and insulting name—he
  captured Helenos by trickery,
  coming upon him alone and at night.
  Taking him prisoner, he showed him off in fetters to
    the Achaians   620
  —a lovely quarry, indeed.

  Helenos prophesied everything to them,
  how they would never capture the citadel of Troy,
  if they did not persuade this man and bring him
  back from the island where he lives now.

  And as soon as the son of Laertes heard the seer
    say this,
  he immediately announced to the Achaians that he
    would bring the man back
  and show him to them;
  that the man would likely come freely,
  but if not, then he would bring him against his will. 630
  And that, should he fail to accomplish this,
  let any one who wants to
  have his head.

  Now you've heard everything.
  I advise you to make haste, you and anyone whom
    you care about.

PHILOCTETES That man—he is nothing but damage! He swore
             he'd *persuade* and bring me to the Achaians?
             I shall, I suppose, be persuaded when I'm dead
             to come up from Hades and into the light, like *his*
                  father—

TRADER I don't know about any of that—   640
        I'm going to the ship. And may the gods bring all
             the best.
                              Exit TRADER *and his companion.*

PHILOCTETES Is it not terrible, child,
             that the son of Laertes would hope by softening words
             to lead me to his ship, and then display me in the
                  midst of the Argives?

             No—I'd rather listen to what I hate most,
             the serpent that made of my foot a useless thing.
                                                      —But

             that man is capable of saying and daring anything—
             and now I know he'll come.

             Let us go,   650
             that a great sea may separate us from the ship of
                  Odysseus.
             Let's go—
             timely haste at the hour of need has been known to
                  bring sleep
             and relief, later.

NEOPTOLEMOS Fine—when the wind eases off of the prow, we'll
                  set out.
             But at the moment, it's against us.

PHILOCTETES When fleeing evils, the sailing is always good.

NEOPTOLEMOS I know—but the wind is also against *them*—

PHILOCTETES The wind is never against pirates,
          when there's a chance to rob and to seize by force.   660

NEOPTOLEMOS Then if it seems best, let's go—take from within
          whatever you need and want.

PHILOCTETES There *are* some necessary things, though not in great
          supply.

NEOPTOLEMOS What can there be, that isn't on my ship?

PHILOCTETES I have an herb, with which I always dress this wound;
          it eases the pain.

NEOPTOLEMOS Well, bring it—And what else will you take?

PHILOCTETES Any of these arrows of mine that may have fallen
          around here,
    and gone unnoticed—
    I won't leave them for anyone else to take.

                  Brings from his cave a clump of herbs, arrows,
                                    and his long bow.

NEOPTOLEMOS And what is it you're holding now—
          is *that* the famed bow?   670

PHILOCTETES This is it—there's no other, save this which I bear in
          my hands.

NEOPTOLEMOS May I look at it more closely—and hold it—
          worship it, even, as I would a god?

PHILOCTETES For you, not only this bow but
          anything else in my power to give
          will be yours.

NEOPTOLEMOS Indeed, I desire it, but in this way—if it is the gods'
          will,

yes, I wish it;
but if it isn't, then never mind.

PHILOCTETES Your words are blameless—and yes, it   680
              is right, by the gods:
              you alone have enabled me to look upon the light of
                  the sun,
              to see Oita again, and my old father, my kin. You
              have raised me up when I lay beneath the heel of my
                  enemies.
              Be confident—you may touch it,
              then give it back to me,
              and boast that to you, of all mortals, because of your
                  kindness,
              it was granted to touch it.
              For I myself first acquired it by doing a kindness.

NEOPTOLEMOS I don't regret at all knowing you and having you as
                  a friend.   690
              For whoever, in enjoying a kindness,
              knows how to return one as well—he is a friend
              more valuable than any possession. Go inside.

PHILOCTETES I shall have you accompany me,
              for the disease makes me need you for support.

              NEOPTOLEMOS, *holding the bow, supports* PHILOCTETES
                            as they enter the cave together.

CHORUS I have heard the story,   *strophe*
          but have never seen the legendary intruder on the
              marriage bed,
          he whom the all-powerful son of Kronos made
          prisoner upon a revolving wheel in Hades.

          But I have known neither by hearsay nor as witness   700
          any man, of all mortals,
          with a more hateful fate than this man,

who has done no harm to anyone,
has killed no one, but—a just man to
those who are also just—
has long been perishing undeservedly.

What amazes me is this—
how it is, how in the world, when
all alone, hearing
nothing but the waves always   710
crashing, how he managed to endure a life so full
        of tears.

He was all by himself, had   *antistrophe*
no one who might approach him,
for there was no other inhabitant,
no neighbor in his misery
with whom, in mutual agonies, he could
bewail his slow-murdering, flesh-eating disease.

None who might help him, with soothing herbs, to
find sleep, some respite from the hot, oozing
blood of his foot's wounds in their wild   720
festering—

no one who might come to him with food gathered
from the nourishing earth.

But here and there, instead, he made his way,
crawling, like a child without its dear nurse, toward
whatever source of ease might arise,
whenever the wasting disease happened to let up.

Taking no food—   *strophe*
not, at least, by the sowing of the sacred earth—
nor anything else that   730
laboring men enjoy, except when he was able to
bring down with the winged arrows of his quick bow
some food for his belly.

A wretched life,
which for ten years has not known the pleasure
of even a drink of wine—
no,
no sooner might he see a pool of stagnant water,
he'd approach it.

But now,   *antistrophe*   740
he has come upon the son of noble men,
and will attain good fortune, and
greatness, as a result.
For his rescuer intends to bring him
by sea-crossing ship, over many months,
to his ancestral home, home of the Melian nymphs,
along the banks of Spercheios,
where Herakles of the bronze shield
drew near to the gods,
a god himself,   750
radiant in holy fire, beyond the hills of Oita.

> NEOPTOLEMOS *and* PHILOCTETES *emerge*
> *from the lower cave.*

NEOPTOLEMOS Come. Why are you silent, not speaking, as if
struck into silence by something?

PHILOCTETES   *Lets out a scream.*

NEOPTOLEMOS What is it?

PHILOCTETES Nothing terrible—come.

NEOPTOLEMOS It isn't the pain of your sickness coming upon you,
                        is it?

PHILOCTETES Not at all—on the contrary, I feel like I'm rallying,
                        just now—Oh, gods!—

NEOPTOLEMOS Why do you call upon the gods and groan like that?

PHILOCTETES So that they'll come to us as kind protectors.   760

> *Suddenly screams again.*

NEOPTOLEMOS What are you suffering from?

PHILOCTETES *remains silent in a paroxysm of pain.*

Won't you speak?
You seem to be in trouble.

PHILOCTETES I am all but dying, child; I can't hide my agony from
            you—ah,
            it goes through, is piercing straight through me, and
            I am
            miserable—half-dead—I am being devoured—

            Oh, by the gods themselves, if you have a sword
            handy,
            cut my foot off, as quickly as possible,
            cut it off,   770
            never mind my life—

            do it!

NEOPTOLEMOS What is it now? What
            causes you to raise such shouts and groans?

PHILOCTETES But—you know already.

NEOPTOLEMOS What?

PHILOCTETES You *know*.

NEOPTOLEMOS What is wrong with you? I *don't* know!

PHILOCTETES How can you *not* know?

                                    Shrieking suddenly.

NEOPTOLEMOS The burden of the disease must indeed be fearsome.   780

PHILOCTETES Fearsome—untellable—But—
Have mercy on me.

NEOPTOLEMOS What shall I do?

PHILOCTETES Don't be afraid and—don't betray me—
the disease—its attacks—arrive at various times,
when they've had their fill, I suppose, of wandering
elsewhere.

NEOPTOLEMOS Oh, you are
wretched indeed, clearly wretched in all your
suffering.
Would you like me to hold you—to hold you close?

PHILOCTETES Not at all—no! But take the bow you asked me for
just now—   790
and, until the present pain of the disease eases off,
guard it,
protect it.
For sleep overtakes me, whenever this pain would
leave—it
cannot leave
before then.
So you must let me sleep in peace.
And if *those* people show up in the meantime,
I beg you:
do not give the bow to anyone, willingly or
unwillingly,   800
lest you end up killing yourself
and me, your suppliant.

NEOPTOLEMOS Don't worry. It'll be given to none but you and me.
Give it to me—and here's to luck!

PHILOCTETES Here, take it—but offer a prayer to avert the gods'
envy,
so the bow won't destroy you,
as it did me, and the one who owned it before me.

65

NEOPTOLEMOS Dear gods, let these things be granted us—
and that our voyage may be swift and favorable,
to wherever the god deems just and   810
as the mission itself dictates.

PHILOCTETES   *Shouts in agony.*

Child—
I fear your prayer goes unfulfilled—
for even now, the bloody wound is dripping,
the blood oozes from somewhere deep,
and I half-predict some new development—ah—
my foot, what agonies you cause me!
The pain, it
creeps forward—   820
it's coming nearer—ah,   ah,   ah—!

You understand.   Don't run away.   *Shrieks.*

Oh, Odysseus,
would that this pain might run you straight through
          your chest!
And—

                              Again shrieking in agony.

And you two generals, Agamemnon, Menelaos:
if only instead of me
you might nourish this sickness, for as long a time!

Oh   my . . .   *Sudden cry of pain.*   830

Death—Death—
how is it that, though you are called upon each day,
you can never come?

Son—noble one—take me up
and burn me in the fire called Lemnian—
please—as

66

I myself agreed to do for the son of Zeus,
in exchange for these arms, over which you now stand
            guard—

What do you say, my friend?
What do you say? Why silent? Where are you?   840

NEOPTOLEMOS For some time, now, I've been in pain for you,
grieving over your sufferings.

PHILOCTETES But be assured that the pains come to me suddenly,
            and
as swiftly depart. Only—
I beg you—
don't leave me here alone.

NEOPTOLEMOS Don't worry—I'll stay with you.

PHILOCTETES You'll stay?

NEOPTOLEMOS Yes, of course.

PHILOCTETES I don't think it's fitting for you to swear an oath—but   850

NEOPTOLEMOS It isn't right that I go *without* you.

PHILOCTETES With your hand, make a pledge.

NEOPTOLEMOS I promise to stay with you.

PHILOCTETES   *Looking up to the rock platform and higher*
                                        entrance to the cave.

There now—over there—

NEOPTOLEMOS What are you saying? Where?

PHILOCTETES Up—

67

NEOPTOLEMOS   *Grabbing hold of* PHILOCTETES.

What—Are you turning delirious again?
Why are you looking up at the sky?

PHILOCTETES Let me—

Let me go.   860

NEOPTOLEMOS Where to?

PHILOCTETES Anywhere, just let go of me.

NEOPTOLEMOS I won't.

PHILOCTETES You'll destroy me, if you touch me.

NEOPTOLEMOS All right, I'm letting go of you, now that you're
                    thinking a bit more clearly.

PHILOCTETES Oh Earth, dead as I am, take me—
                    for this agony no longer even lets me stand up.
                                                    Collapses.

NEOPTOLEMOS   *To the* CHORUS.
                    I think sleep will soon come to him:
                    his head is stretched back;
                    and a sweat drips from his entire body;   870
                    and a dark vein, bleeding violently, has broken from
                              the bottom of his foot.
                    Let's allow him some peace, friends, so he can fall
                              asleep.

CHORUS Sleep, ignorant of agony, of grief   *strophe*
                    ignorant, Sleep—may you come to us
                    like a sweet breeze, full of blessing, lord—blessing us.
                    Hold over his eyes this flashing light
                    which stands over them now.
                    Come to me—Oh, healing one, come!

Child, watch where you stand,
where you walk,   880
take thought for what is next—
for already, you can see how . . .
Why are we waiting to take action?
Timely action, which holds sway in all things,
wins great victory when paired with swiftness.

NEOPTOLEMOS But this man hears nothing. And anyway, as I see it,
we capture our quarry—his bow—in vain, if we sail
    without him.
For the victor's garland is not the bow, but Philoctetes—
the gods said we should bring *him*.
To boast, with lies, of deeds that remain undone   890
is disgraceful.

CHORUS But the god will see to these things.   *antistrophe*
Answer me, quietly,
give me, however brief, some answer.
For in sickness, sleep is sleepless,
sharpsighted,
sees everything.
But whatever you are most capable of,
that thing,
whatever it is, see to it that you do it secretly.   900
You know whom I'm speaking of.

But if you share his opinion in this matter,
the problems are unresolvable, baffling
even to the wise.

A wind, child; a wind—   *epode*
The man is sightless, helpless,
lies as if shrouded in night—a good sleep is
    without fear—
and he commands no hand or foot or
—or anything else, but lies
like someone on the threshold of Hades.   910
Look, and see whether what you say

is timely; this much I can grasp:
those efforts most succeed, which know no fear.

NEOPTOLEMOS Be silent, and don't lose your heads.
⸱   For he moves his eyes now—he's raising his head.

PHILOCTETES Oh light that follows sleep, and—
beyond my hopes—watch kept by these strangers!
For I could never even have prayed for this:
that you would have pity on and endure my agonies
        and
stay with me and—help me.   920
The Atreidai certainly didn't manage to do as much,
noble generals that they are!
But yours is a noble nature, born of those in
turn of noble nature—
all my suffering you found manageable,
my shouting, my foul smell.
And now, since there seems to be a moment of
forgetfulness and ease to this sickness,
come and lift me, help me up,
so that when the tiredness leaves me a bit more,
        we can   930
set off for the ship and soon be sailing.

NEOPTOLEMOS It's good to see you, beyond what I'd hoped,
free of pain, looking about yourself, breathing still.
For it had seemed that, in your agonies,
you had left us.
But now, get up.
Or, if you'd rather,
these men will carry you. They won't mind the labor,
since you and I have agreed on what's best.

PHILOCTETES I thank you for that.   940
Now—if you'd lift me, as you intended.
Let these men go for now, so they won't grow
        oppressed too soon
by my terrible stench—

for there will be effort enough to suffice them, when
    I'm on the ship.

NEOPTOLEMOS Fine, then; stand up, and hold on.

PHILOCTETES Don't worry—long habit will raise me up.

NEOPTOLEMOS Alas—what should I do next?

PHILOCTETES What is it? Where are your words headed?

NEOPTOLEMOS My speech is aimless, I don't know
    where to turn it.   950

PHILOCTETES Why are you at a loss? Don't say this.

NEOPTOLEMOS But that's just where I've come to in this troublesome
    business.

PHILOCTETES Has the burden of my sickness persuaded you
    not to take me aboard, after all?

NEOPTOLEMOS Everything is burdensome,
    when—taking leave of his very nature,
    a man does what he knows hardly befits him.

PHILOCTETES But—in helping a noble man,
    you neither do nor say anything that your own father
      wouldn't have said.

NEOPTOLEMOS I shall be seen as disgraceful—this, for some time, has
    been my agony.   960

PHILOCTETES Certainly not from anything you've done—
    but what you say,
    it frightens me.

NEOPTOLEMOS O Zeus, what shall I do?
    Am I to be found evil on two counts—

hiding that which I ought not to,
and saying what is most shameful?

PHILOCTETES This man, if I judge correctly, acts like one who
has already betrayed and abandoned me,
and is about to set sail.   970

NEOPTOLEMOS Not abandoning you—rather,
sending you on what will prove grievous to you—
it's this that has long pained me.

PHILOCTETES What are you saying?—I don't understand.

NEOPTOLEMOS I won't lie to you: you must sail to Troy—
to the Achaians and the mission of the Atreidai.

PHILOCTETES What?! What do you mean?

NEOPTOLEMOS Do not groan, before you've understood everything.

PHILOCTETES What's to be understood?
What do you intend to do to me?   980

NEOPTOLEMOS First, to rescue you from your misfortune;
then—together with you—to go and sack Troy.

PHILOCTETES Is it true—these things—that you intend to do them?

NEOPTOLEMOS A great necessity demands it. Listen, and don't get
angry.

PHILOCTETES I am damned—betrayed!
Stranger, why,
why have you done this?
Give me back my bow immediately!

NEOPTOLEMOS That isn't possible. Both justice and expediency force
me to obey those in command.

PHILOCTETES You fire—you absolute horror, you most hateful
                     strategem of terrible outrage—   990
              what things you've done to me,
              how you've cheated me!
              Are you not ashamed to look at me here at your feet,
                     a suppliant to you,
              yourself shameful?

              In seizing my bow, you have snatched, too, my life.
              Give it to me—I beg you—give it back—
              please—

              By the gods of your fathers, do not rob me of my life.

              —But he no longer speaks to me; he looks as if
              he will never return it to me again.   1000

              Oh harbors,
              oh headlands,
              oh mountain beasts in packs, oh rugged rocks—
              for I know none other to speak to except
              you who have always been here with me—
              to you I speak
              of what the son of Achilles has done to me.
              Having sworn to bring me home,
              he instead drives me to Troy;
              having offered his right hand in pledge,   1010
              he has seized and holds onto my bow,
              the sacred bow of Herakles, son of Zeus!

              And he wants to show me off to the Argives
              as if having overpowered a strong man,
              he drives me by force, when in fact he kills a man
              dead already,
              a skein of smoke,
              a mere specter.
              For he wouldn't have taken me, had I been a
                     strong man—
              nor even in my present condition, if not by trickery.   1020

But now I have been miserably deceived—
what should I do?—

Give it back!

Even now, come to your senses.
What do you say?

You're silent. And I—I
exist no longer.

Double-mouthed cave,
again—after so long—I return to you,
stripped of all means of living—   1030
I shall wither away, alone, in this dwelling,
bringing down with this bow no winged bird, no
mountain-grazing beast—
but I myself, dying miserably, shall provide the food
for those whom once I fed on;
and those whom I once hunted—
they will now hunt me.
Ah, I shall make slaughter the reprisal for slaughter,
because of one who seemed to know nothing of evil.

Turning to NEOPTOLEMOS.

May you die!—but not before I learn   1040
if you've changed your mind again; if not,
may you die miserably!

CHORUS What shall we do?
It is up to you, my lord—
whether we should set sail already;
whether, instead, to agree with what this man says.

NEOPTOLEMOS Not now for the first time, no—
it has long been the case: a terrible pity for this
        man has
broken upon me.

PHILOCTETES Have mercy on me, child—by the gods!—   1050
            and do not prove yourself an object of shame
                        among men,
            for having deceived me.

NEOPTOLEMOS What shall I do?
             Better never to have left Skyros, I am that
             wrenched by this business.

PHILOCTETES You are not evil. But,
             in having learned from men who *are* evil,
             you seem to have arrived at a disgraceful situation.
             Give to others what is proper:
             sail away,   1060
             but give my weapons back to me.

NEOPTOLEMOS Men, what shall I do?—

                        ODYSSEUS *and some sailors suddenly enter from*
                                        the side of the stage.
                        ODYSSEUS *addresses* NEOPTOLEMOS.

ODYSSEUS You traitor! What are you doing?
          Come back here and give me that bow!

PHILOCTETES Who is that? Not Odysseus—is it?

ODYSSEUS Odysseus indeed—I myself, whom you can see!

PHILOCTETES I've been bought
             —and sold.
             He it was, then, who captured me—
             who stripped me of my weapons!   1070

ODYSSEUS It certainly was—I, and nobody else—I do confess it.

PHILOCTETES   *To* NEOPTOLEMOS.

             Hand the bow back to me—give it back!

75

ODYSSEUS This—even should he wish to—he shall never do.
But you must come with the bow—
or these men will bring you by force.

PHILOCTETES You worst and most outrageous of evil men—

Pointing to Odysseus's men.

these men will drive me by force?

ODYSSEUS Yes—if you don't come willingly.

PHILOCTETES O land of Lemnos, and all-powerful flame forged by
Hephaistos,
must I endure this too?   1080
that this man shall drive me by force from this island?

ODYSSEUS It is Zeus—if you must know—
Zeus, the ruler of this land,
by Zeus himself that these things have been
determined—
I merely serve him.

PHILOCTETES Hateful one, what lies you've found to say.
You put the gods before you like a shield, and in
so doing,
you make of the gods liars.

ODYSSEUS No—it is the truth—and this road must be traveled.

PHILOCTETES No!   1090

ODYSSEUS Yes! You've no choice but to obey.

PHILOCTETES Ah, then I am damned indeed.
Clearly, my father sired no free man, but a slave.

ODYSSEUS No—neither of these.
Rather, a man equal to the noblest men,
and you are to sack and utterly demolish Troy.

PHILOCTETES Never! Not even if it means I must suffer every evil—
so long as I still have my cliff here.

ODYSSEUS And what will you do?

PHILOCTETES   *Looking up to the rock platform, then limping*
                                                     toward it.
I shall throw myself from the rocks above,   1100
and dash my head on the rocks below me.

ODYSSEUS   *To his men.*
Seize him! Don't let him do it!

PHILOCTETES Oh hands of mine—hunted down by this man—
what things you suffer now, companionless,
no bow.

And you, Odysseus—you who think nothing healthy
        or noble—
how you crept up to me,
how you hunted me,
taking as shield for yourself this boy, a stranger to me
—himself unworthy of you, though worthy of myself—   1110
he who knew nothing but to obey an order.
And now
how he suffers for his mistakes, for what
I've endured.

But your evil soul, looking always out from its
        innermost chambers,
taught him well—
this child with no natural gift for it,
and with no will for it—
taught him to be skilled in evil.

And now, you wretch, you mean to shackle and   1120
lead me from the very shore where
once you left me alone with no friend,
with no city—
a corpse for the wild animals—
May you die!
How often I've prayed for your death.

But the gods, it seems, have nothing sweet in mind
        for me:
for you have managed to live,
while I suffer all over again the fate of living
wretchedly among so many evils,   1130
to be mocked by the sons of Atreus
and you, their lackey.

And yet,
you sailed with them after being yoked by kidnapping
        and necessity;
whereas I, all the worse for me,
willingly sailed as captain of seven ships—
it is *they* who, according to you, cast me off in
        dishonor,
though they blame *you*.

But why are you taking me now?
Why?   1140
To what advantage?
I, who am nothing now, am long since dead to you.
Most hateful to the gods,
why don't I seem lame and stinking to you, now?
How will you be able to burn sacrifices to the gods,
if I sail with you? How make libation?
For this was exactly why you threw me out, as you
        said then.

May you die miserably!
You *will* die, for having wronged a man like me,
if there is any justice among the gods.   1150

78

And I know there *is*:
for you would never have sailed on a mission such
        as this
for a man so worthless as myself—not unless
some spur of the gods had driven you to it.

But—oh fatherland and protecting gods—
punish them in due time,
punish all of them,
if you have any pity for me.
For I live pitiably,
but if I could see these men destroyed,   1160
it would be as if I'd escaped my disease itself!

CHORUS Grave is this stranger, Odysseus, and he makes a
            speech as grave,
        one that does not give at all in
        to his sufferings.

ODYSSEUS I'd have much to say in response to his words, if
            I could.
        But for now, I can say only one thing:
        where a man is needed, of whatever kind, I am
            such a man;
        if the time called for just and upright men,
        you would find no one more noble than myself.
        However, I was born desiring absolute victory—   1170

        except when it comes to you; now, willingly, I shall
            yield to you.

                                        To his men.

        Release him, hold him no longer!
        Let him stay.
        After all, Teucer is with us—he has the skill of
            archery—
        as do I: I don't think I'm any worse than you at
        mastering this bow, nor any worse a hand at
            taking aim.

We have the arms now—who needs you?
Farewell—
and enjoy strolling around Lemnos!

        PHILOCTETES *is released by Odysseus's men.*

Let's go. Perhaps they'll honor me with your prized
    possession—   1180
you ought to have held onto it.

PHILOCTETES Oh what shall I do in my misery?
Are you to appear before the Argives adorned in
    weapons that are mine?

ODYSSEUS Enough talk—I'm leaving.

PHILOCTETES Son of Achilles—
Have *you* nothing to say to me?
Are *you* leaving, like this?

ODYSSEUS You come here, Neoptolemos!—and don't look
    at him!
Being so noble, you're liable to wreck our good
    fortune.

PHILOCTETES Am I to be left alone by you in this way, strangers?   1190
Will you not pity me?

CHORUS This young man is our captain. What he says,
    we say also.

NEOPTOLEMOS Odysseus will say that I am too full of pity—all the
    same, men,
stay—if it is all right with him—
for as much time as is needed for the sailors to
    prepare the ship,
and for us to pray to the gods.
And perhaps this one (*pointing to* PHILOCTETES) will
    think better of us in this matter.
Therefore, let us set off—

And you, men, when we call, you set off quickly
    as well.

NEOPTOLEMOS *and* ODYSSEUS *exit.*

PHILOCTETES O hollow cavern—   *strophe* 1200
    hot sometimes; sometimes, like ice—
    so I was never meant to leave you;
    no, you will be with me in my dying.

    O sorry dwelling, filled
    entirely with my suffering,
    what life shall I have again, day to day?
    What hope of finding food,
    where find it?
    You creatures flying above, who once feared me,
    come now through the sharp wind—   1210
    I am powerless, at last, to catch you.

CHORUS Yours is a hard lot,
    but it is you who have damned yourself—
    this fate came from nowhere else, from no greater
        source than you.
    For when it was possible to have sense,
    when a better fate was possible,
    you chose the worse one.

PHILOCTETES I am miserable—   *antistrophe*
    I am wretched—and torn by my hardship: in
    living henceforward with no one else in my misery,   1220
    I shall die finding no food for myself,
    my hands powerless to do so
    without my weapons—their wings, their speed.

    Unseen, hidden,
    the words of a deceitful mind
    have overtaken me. May I live to see
    the man behind those words

suffer as I have, and
for as long.

CHORUS The destiny of the gods has brought this on you—   1230
no deceit of mine;
send elsewhere your hate,
your curse of a prayer.
I am worried that your friendship
may leave me.

PHILOCTETES Somewhere, sitting   *strophe*
on this grey ocean's beach, he makes
mock of me, brandishing in his hand
my means of living, which
none before, ever, had even touched.   1240

Dear bow,
wrested from hands as dear,
I'm sure if you have
any conscious feelings, you look with
pity on the wretched heir to Herakles, who won't ever
again use you, no—
                    instead, you'll
be handled by a schemer's hands,
witness to disgraceful deceits, and to a man
hateful,   1250
hated,
bringing about a thousand deeds of shame—
he brought as much on me.

CHORUS It is right for a man to say what is just—
but having said it, for his tongue
not to put forward hate and pain.
For this man is one of many who,
at the command of another,
has brought about what is best
overall   1260
for his friends.

PHILOCTETES O beasts—winged, bright-eyed,   *antistrophe*
mountain-feeding—
all who dwell here:
no longer will you rush in flight from
your dwelling-places; for I no longer
hold in my hands the former protection
of my arrows—

                    But come boldly—
You'll find me lame, no longer   1270
a source of fear for you—how
lovely, now, to satisfy your mouths upon
this, my discolored flesh.
For I shall die at once—
where, after all, will my livelihood come from?
Who can live in this way, upon the winds,
when he no longer has possession
of anything that the life-sustaining
earth sends forth?

CHORUS By the gods—if you honor anything at all,   1280
approach the visitor,
who has himself approached you with all good
          intention.
Consider,
and understand clearly:
it is possible for you to escape this fate;
for it is pitiable, how it feeds on you,
and he who lives with such suffering has no notion of
          how to bear it.

PHILOCTETES Again, you remind me of my old agony—
you, who are the best of all those who have come
          here before—
Why have you destroyed me? Why are you doing this
          to me?   1290

CHORUS Why do you say this?

PHILOCTETES   Because you hoped to drive me to the hated land
     of Troy.

CHORUS   But I think this is best.

PHILOCTETES   Leave me—now!

CHORUS   What you've commanded is fine with me—
    I am pleased to do it.
    Let's go—
    off to our assigned places on board our ship!

PHILOCTETES   *Shouting.*
    Don't go—by the Zeus of prayer and curse—I beg
    you.

CHORUS   Easy—   1300

PHILOCTETES   *Shouting.*
    Strangers,
    by the gods—stay here.

CHORUS   What are you shouting about?

PHILOCTETES   The god, the god,
    destiny,
    destiny—;
    my foot;
    how shall I live from now on?

    Strangers: come back.

CHORUS   And do what?   1310
    You seem of a different mind than before.

PHILOCTETES   There's no need to hate a man who, torn by suffering,
    says something counter to what makes sense.

CHORUS   Wretched one—come now, as we've told you to do.

PHILOCTETES Never—never! Get this clear:
not even if the fire-bearing wielder of
lightning should come consuming me in its blaze!
Let Troy perish,
and all those beneath it,
who dared to banish my foot, and me with it!   1320

But strangers, grant me at least one prayer.

CHORUS What is it?

PHILOCTETES Provide me with a sword, if there's one about—
or an ax,
even an arrow.

CHORUS What for?

PHILOCTETES To cut off my head and all my limbs—
murder,
slaughter's my intention!

CHORUS But why?   1330

PHILOCTETES That I might see again my father.

CHORUS Where—in what country?

PHILOCTETES That of Hades.
For he is no longer here, in the light.
O city—
paternal city,
if only I might see you, wretched though I am,
who left your holy stream and
as an ally
went with the hateful Greeks, and now   1340
I am nothing at all.

CHORUS By now I'd be long since en route to my ship,
       if I didn't see in the distance
       Odysseus and the son of Achilles coming back to us.

PHILOCTETES *returns to his cave.* ODYSSEUS *arrives on
stage and confronts* NEOPTOLEMOS, *who is carrying the
bow of Philoctetes.*

ODYSSEUS Won't you tell me why you're headed back in this
         way, and so quickly?

NEOPTOLEMOS To undo the wrong I did earlier.

ODYSSEUS You're speaking strangely—
         what wrong did you commit?

NEOPTOLEMOS The wrong of obeying you and all of the Greek army.

ODYSSEUS What have you done that wasn't appropriate to you?   1350

NEOPTOLEMOS I took a man by deceit, by shameful trickery.

ODYSSEUS What man?
         You aren't planning something new, are you?

NEOPTOLEMOS Nothing new—but to the son of Poias—

ODYSSEUS What? What will you do?
         A strange fear has come over me.

NEOPTOLEMOS He from whom I took this bow,
            to him again—

ODYSSEUS Zeus—
         what are you saying?   1360
         You don't intend to give it back, do you?

NEOPTOLEMOS Yes, for I only have it by having taken it
            shamefully and unjustly.

ODYSSEUS By the gods, are you saying this as a joke?

NEOPTOLEMOS Only if it is a joke to speak the truth.

ODYSSEUS What are you saying, son of Achilles?
What do you mean?

NEOPTOLEMOS Do you want me to say the same thing twice—
three times?

ODYSSEUS I'd rather have heard nothing from the start!

NEOPTOLEMOS Be clear on this point: you've heard everything.   1370

ODYSSEUS But there is someone—
someone who will prevent you from doing this.

NEOPTOLEMOS What are you saying? Who will stop me?

ODYSSEUS The entire army of the Achaians—and I,
among them.

NEOPTOLEMOS Though you were born clever, you manage to
speak stupidly.

ODYSSEUS Well, in your case,
both words and actions lack intelligence.

NEOPTOLEMOS But if these things are just, they outweigh what is
clever.

ODYSSEUS And how is it just for
you to give back what you took thanks to   1380
my planning?

NEOPTOLEMOS I shall attempt to undo a wrong that was shameful.

ODYSSEUS Don't you fear the Greek army, in doing this?

NEOPTOLEMOS Since I'm in the right,
no,
I don't fear your army.
Nor shall I be persuaded to do anything by force.

ODYSSEUS Then it's not with the Trojans, but with *you*
we'll fight!

NEOPTOLEMOS Let that be as it will.

ODYSSEUS Do you see my right hand clasping the hilt of
my sword?   1390

NEOPTOLEMOS Then see *my* hand
at *my* sword.

ODYSSEUS Fine—I'll leave you to yourself.
But I plan to go and tell this to the entire army.
They will punish you.

NEOPTOLEMOS You've thought wisely.
And should you think this way
from now on, perhaps you'll manage to stay out
of trouble.

ODYSSEUS *exits.* NEOPTOLEMOS *approaches the cave.*

But you, son of Poias—Philoctetes,
come here, out of your rocky dwelling.   1400

PHILOCTETES What is all this shouting near the cave?
Why are you calling me to come out?
What do you need?
—Something bad, I am sure.
You aren't here—are you?—to
bring me some great trouble on top of my other
suffering?

NEOPTOLEMOS Don't worry. Listen to the words I've brought you.

PHILOCTETES I am frightened.
             I was ruined before by lovely words—your words—
             when I was persuaded by them.   1410

NEOPTOLEMOS Can't I change my mind again?

PHILOCTETES You were no different in speech
             when you stole my bow from me—
             trustworthy,
             yet secretly ruinous.

NEOPTOLEMOS But not now—
             I wish to hear from you what
             you've decided:
             will you stay here and live out your life,
             or sail with us?   1420

PHILOCTETES Stop—don't speak any further!
             For whatever you say, it will all be said in vain.

NEOPTOLEMOS Is that your decision?

PHILOCTETES As much, anyway, as words alone can say.

NEOPTOLEMOS I'd like to have persuaded you with my words—
             but if what I say is useless in this matter,
             well, then I am finished.

PHILOCTETES All that you say *is* useless.
             For you will never find me generous-minded
                  toward you,
             who stripped me of what kept me alive!   1430
             And then you come advising me—
             you, the hateful son of a noble father!
             May you die, all of you—first the Atreidai,
             and then the son of Laertes—
             and then you!

89

NEOPTOLEMOS No more cursing—
      here, take this weapon of yours from my right hand.

PHILOCTETES What are you saying?
      Am I being deceived a second time?

NEOPTOLEMOS No—I swear it,   1440
      by holy reverence for highest Zeus.

PHILOCTETES If what you say is the truth, you say what is most
      welcome to me.

NEOPTOLEMOS The act itself is clear. Here—
      put your right hand out, and take possession of your
        weapons.

                                     ODYSSEUS *enters.*

ODYSSEUS I forbid it!—with the gods as my witnesses,
      and on behalf of the Atreidai and the entire army!

PHILOCTETES Whose voice do I hear? Not that of Odysseus, I hope?

ODYSSEUS It *is*, in fact. You see me here—
      the one who will drive you by force to Troy,   1450
      whether the son of Achilles wishes it or not!

PHILOCTETES You won't rejoice in anything, if this arrow finds
      its mark!

NEOPTOLEMOS   *Grabbing* PHILOCTETES.
      Ah no, by the gods, don't shoot your arrow!

PHILOCTETES By the gods, let go of my hands, dearest child!

NEOPTOLEMOS I won't!

PHILOCTETES Why—why did you prevent me from
      killing this man—my hated enemy—with my bow?

NEOPTOLEMOS But killing isn't right for either of us.

PHILOCTETES Well, this much is clear: the leaders of the army,
the false messengers of the Achaians, are no good
             at war   1460
—however bold they may be with their words.

NEOPTOLEMOS That may be so. But you have your bow,
and no reason to be angry with
or blame me.

PHILOCTETES Child, I agree; you have made evident
the stock from which you were born—
not that of Sisyphos as a father, but of Achilles,
who held the greatest nobility when he was among
             the living—
and now too, among the dead.

                              ODYSSEUS *leaves abruptly.*

NEOPTOLEMOS I am pleased to hear you speak well of my father—   1470
of him and of myself.
But now, listen to what I ask of you.

Men must bear the fortune
given them by the gods. But
those who are set upon by
damage that is of their own doing,
such as yourself,
it is just neither to have sympathy for them, nor to
             pity them.
You have become an animal, and refuse
all advice: if someone, thinking on your behalf,   1480
does give advice, you hate him, you
consider him an enemy.

Nevertheless, I shall speak,
calling upon the Zeus of oath-making.
Consider this—and write it deeply into your mind.

You are sick with this disease by divine will.
For you came close to Chryse and
the unseen serpent who keeps watch
over that roofless shrine.
There is never to be any respite   1490
from this grave infection—so long as the same
    sun rises
here, and sets there—
until you come willingly to Troy,
and, meeting the sons of Asklepios,
you will be cured of disease,
and will be proven with me and with your bow to be
Troy's destruction.

As to how I know these things are the case,
I shall tell you.
A man from Troy was captured by us—Helenos,   1500
the best of seers—who has said clearly
these things must happen.
And more—
that all Troy must be taken this summer.
He has agreed to be put to death, should he prove to
    be a liar.
Therefore, knowing this, come willingly.
For it is wonderful, to be judged the best of
    the Greeks,
to come into healing hands, and
then, in sacking Troy,
to bring upon yourself the highest fame.   1510

PHILOCTETES Hateful Life,
    why do you still hold me alive
    and seeing?
    Why won't you let me go to Hades?

    What shall I do? How
    not to believe the words of this man
    who has advised me with my best interests in mind?

Am I to yield, then?

But, in doing so, how shall I
in my misfortune come into the light?   1520
Who will speak to me?

To the CHORUS.

You, who stand around me and see all of this:
how will you stand for it, my joining the sons of Atreus,
who destroyed me,
my joining the ruinous son of Laertes?

For it isn't the pain of what has happened before
that bites at me; rather, it is what I can see
I will have to suffer in the future.
For those whose mind becomes a mother of evil,
this mind will mother other evils still.   1530

To NEOPTOLEMOS.

You amaze me:
you ought not to go to Troy,
and you should keep me from it, as well.
After all, these men insulted you
by depriving you of your father's prize —
will you now be an ally to them, and force
me to be one also?
Hardly!

But as you swore to me before,
send me home. As for yourself,   1540
stay in Skyros, and let these cruel men be
cruelly destroyed.
Thus will you gain from me and my father, both,
a double favor.
And, in not helping the wicked, you will make it
      clear that
you aren't among the wicked yourself.

NEOPTOLEMOS What you say is reasonable; nevertheless,
I want you to trust the gods and my words,
and with me as your friend, sail from this land.

PHILOCTETES To Troy   1550
and to the hateful son of Atreus,
on this foot?

NEOPTOLEMOS To those who will relieve from pain both you and
your foot, dripping with pus,
and will save you at last from your disease.

PHILOCTETES You give strange advice—what are you saying?

NEOPTOLEMOS The things that I see will be the best for us both,
if they're done.

PHILOCTETES And in saying this, you feel no shame before the gods?

NEOPTOLEMOS How feel shame, when helping a friend?   1560

PHILOCTETES Do you say this as friend to the Atreidai,
or to me?

NEOPTOLEMOS As *your* friend. Such is my word.

PHILOCTETES How so, if you want to hand me over to my enemies?

NEOPTOLEMOS You should learn, sir, not to be so bold in misfortune.

PHILOCTETES You will destroy me—I know it!—with these words.

NEOPTOLEMOS I won't. You don't understand.

PHILOCTETES Don't I know that the Atreidai exiled me?

NEOPTOLEMOS They exiled you—but now,
see how they would save you.   1570

PHILOCTETES Never, if it means I must willingly see Troy again.

NEOPTOLEMOS What am I to do, if I can't persuade you with what
                        I've said?
                It is time for me to leave this argument,
                and for you to go back to living as you've been living,
                without rescue.

PHILOCTETES Let me suffer what I must.
                And what you swore to me, when you took my right
                        hand—
                to send me home—
                do that for me,
                and don't delay,   1580
                and don't mention Troy again.
                There's been enough talk, already.

NEOPTOLEMOS If that is what seems best,
                let's go.

PHILOCTETES You have spoken nobly!

NEOPTOLEMOS Now steady yourself.

PHILOCTETES As much as I can, I shall.

NEOPTOLEMOS But—how shall I avoid being blamed by
                the Achaians?

PHILOCTETES Don't think about that.

NEOPTOLEMOS But—what if they destroy my country?   1590

PHILOCTETES I shall be there—

NEOPTOLEMOS What help will you render?

PHILOCTETES With the arrows of Herakles—

95

HERAKLES *appears on the rocky ledge at the entry of the*
higher cave.

NEOPTOLEMOS What do you mean?

PHILOCTETES I shall prevent them from approaching!

NEOPTOLEMOS Well, if you will do this, as you say,
then kiss the ground farewell, and come along.

HERAKLES Not yet, son of Poias!
Not until you have heard *my* words.
It is the voice of Herakles you hear,   1600
and his face you see with your eyes.
I have come here from my seat on Olympos,
on your behalf,
and to tell you the plans of Zeus,
and to stop you from this road you are now taking.
Listen to me.

First, I'll remind you of my fortunes,
what sufferings and agonies I
endured before winning the immortal
glory which you see before you.   1610
For you, also — know well — it is fated
that from these sufferings of yours your life
will be made famous.
Going with this man to the city of Troy,
you will find an end to your grievous disease;
of the whole army, you will be declared first in valor,
and with these arrows of mine you will slay
Paris — who was the cause of these troubles —
and you will conquer Troy, and win the best
prizes from the army, and send home the spoils,   1620
to the high plain of your fatherland, Oita,
to your father, Poias.
And whatever spoils you take from this war,
place on my pyre, as tribute to my bow.

I advise the same to you, son of Achilles,
for you aren't strong enough to take Troy
without him, nor he without you.
But each of you must guard the other,
even as two lions that feed together.
Meanwhile, I shall send Asklepios to Troy   1630
to heal your disease. For, once again,
the city is to be taken by my bow.
But remember, when you conquer the land,
to respect what is sacred to the gods.
For father Zeus considers all things
second to this alone.
For reverence does not die with mortals—
whether they live or die, it is never destroyed.

PHILOCTETES Uttering what I've longed for,
you appear at last—   1640
I shall not disregard what you have said.

NEOPTOLEMOS Nor shall I.

HERAKLES Then don't waste time now in
preparing for action—the moment to act
is upon you,
and the wind at your stern.

PHILOCTETES Very well, then. In departing,
I shall call upon this island: farewell,
chamber that kept watch over me,

water-nymphs,   1650

nymphs of the meadows,

the muscled crashing of sea against headland,
where often my head, though
inside the cave, was drenched by the south wind's
        beating,
and often the mountain of Hermes sent

back to me in answer
my own voice
echoing,
groaning,
as I weathered the storm.   1660

But now,
o streams and Lycian spring,
we take leave of you—I leave you
at last,

what I never expected.

Farewell, Lemnos, surrounded by sea—
grant me, free of blame, a safe voyage
to where great Destiny itself
carries me,
and the judgment of my friends,   1670
and the god who tames everything—who himself
        has decreed this.

CHORUS Let us leave together, praying
        to the sea-nymphs,
        that we meet safe voyage home.

                                        Exeunt omnes.

NOTES ON THE TEXT

PROLOGUE 1–178/1–134

3 / 2 *Lemnos* is an island in the northern Aegean just under Mt. Athos, which looms to the north. It is a stage on the way from mainland Greece to the Troad. In Sophocles' time it was an important and inhabited island, and its two main cities (Myrrhine and Hephaistia) were virtually Attic demes. Remarkably, Sophocles makes it an uninhabited island, despite its description in the *Iliad* as being well populated and the realm of the son of Jason and Hypsipyle (*Iliad* 7.467 and 21.40).

7 / 4 *Neoptolemos, son of Achilles* The use of patronymics is remarkable in this play about inherited character. Neoptolemos identifies himself to Philoctetes in the following words: "I am called Neoptolemos, son of Achilles. And now you know everything" (237–38/240–41). Philoctetes is described as the "son of Poias" (9/5) and Odysseus himself is called "son of Laertes," and even of Sisyphos (97/87, and 417/414 with note). The description of Neoptolemos as the son of Achilles initiates one of the major themes of Sophocles' play, that of nature (*physis*), birth, inherited character, and nobility.

9 / 4–5 *The Malian, the son of Poias* Malis is a region to the south of Thessaly occupying the alluvial plain opposite the northern tip of Euboia. In the Homeric Catalogue of Ships (*Iliad* 2.716–28) Philoctetes' home is located in Thessaly, but it migrates to Malis because of his associations with Herakles. Malis is dominated to the south by Mt. Oita, where Herakles was consumed on a pyre. In Sophocles' time, the summit of Oita was the site of a cult of Herakles.

55 / 50 *Son of Achilles* This form of address continues the significant repetition of patronymics in the play and suggests that character passes from father to son without the intervention of education or the influence of society. It is clear that Neoptolemos, born on Skyros, has never seen his father. Odysseus calls him the "son of a noble father" (**105/96**) and Philoctetes says the same as Neoptolemos returns the bow Philoctetes had entrusted to him (**1310–11/1467**).

79 / 72 *You sailed under oath to no one* This oath was the oath taken by the Achaians to avenge the abduction of Helen by Paris; the necessity was the compulsion put upon both Achilles and Odysseus to join the expedition against Troy. According to a tradition on the periphery of the Homeric poems, to avert his death in Troy, Achilles mother, Thetis, disguised her young son as a girl and entrusted him to the care of Lykomedes, King of Skyros, where he stayed among Lykomedes' daughters. There Achilles fell in love with Deidamia, revealed himself as a man, and became the father of Neoptolemos, who was born on the island. In the Book of the Dead of the *Odyssey*, Odysseus tells Achilles that he brought his son, Neoptolemos, from Skyros to Troy, where he distinguished himself in battle and entered the Trojan horse with Odysseus (*Odyssey* 11.506–37).

Odysseus' ruse to avoid service in Troy is the counterpart of Thetis' plan to save her son. To evade joining the expedition against Troy, he pretended that he had gone mad and tried to convince the army of this by plowing the sand of the sea shore, apparently, when he was still on Ithaca. Palamedes (whom Odysseus in revenge accused of treason) revealed his deception by throwing the infant Telemachos in the path of his plow. Odysseus stopped in time and revealed himself as both sane and an imposter. This is the subject of Sophocles' lost *The Madness of Odysseus* (*Odysseus Mainomenos.*)

The "first expedition" to Troy was not that of Herakles against the Troy of Laomedon, the father of Priam, but the expedition of ten years past.

100 / 90 *I'm willing to take the man by force.* According the prophecy of the Trojan seer, Helenos, to assure the capture of Troy Philoctetes had to be brought to Troy "by persuasion" (*logos*, **624/612**). But persuasion, if it involves lying, is disgraceful. Odysseus improves the situation by speaking of deceit (*dolos*), not lying.

109 / 99 *it's the tongue, and not deeds* Odysseus evokes the contrast between word (*logos*) and deed (*ergon*) and the supremacy of word over deed that was part of the sophistic culture of Sophocles' Athens.

126 / 114 *as you said* In Sophocles' Greek, the plural "you said" refers to Odysseus and Phoinix, the tutor of Achilles, who in the later epic tradition were sent to Skyros to fetch Neoptolemos and bring him to Troy after his father had been killed there. Neoptolemos refers to their assurance that he alone would take Troy in 343–47/346–47. In his lying tale, the Trader adds the sons of Theseus to Phoinix in the embassy to Neoptolemos and Skyros (565/562).

129 / 117 *you'll take away two prizes* The prizes Odysseus holds up to Neoptolemos are the combination of intelligence (or, in its debased form, "cleverness") and valor. Among Homer's Achaians, Odysseus is unique in possessing a combination of guile and bravery. Even the young Neoptolemos is capable of speaking well in the deliberations of the Achaian army (*Odyssey* 11.511–12).

145 / 133 *May Hermes the cunning leader* Hermes *dolios* is the much admired patron of merchants, thieves, and tricksters. He began his career by stealing the cattle of his half-brother Apollo and was—at the tender age of one day—brazen enough to deny the theft (Homeric *Hymn to Hermes* 260–77). Among her other attributes, Athena was the goddess of intelligence; she was patron to Odysseus at Troy and, then, in Ithaca at the end of his long voyage home. The elective affinity between the two is brilliantly displayed in their meeting on Ithaca, as Athena disguises herself as a young shepherd and Odysseus tries to conceal his own identity by telling a long lying "Cretan" tale (*Odyssey* 13.222–24 and 254–86).

Athena is called *Polias* (the Goddess of the City), an epithet she does not have in the Homeric poems. In Athens, she is associated with Nike, the Goddess personifying Victory. Athena Polias was one of Athena's cult titles on the Athenian acropolis. Her elegant Ionic temple (of 421 B.C.) built in commemoration of the Athenian victory over the Persians rises to the southwestern entrance to the acropolis. It was dedicated to Apteros Nike (Wingless Victory). Sophocles is clearly forging a connection between Odysseus and Athens.

PARADOS 148–214/135–218

ENTRY OF THE CHORUS

154 / 140 *The divine scepter of Zeus* Sophocles' chorus evokes the scepter symboli-
cally involved in the quarrel between Achilles and Agamemnon in the
Iliad. The *skeptron* of Agamemnon is described as a hereditary possession fashioned by Hephaistos and given by Zeus to Pelops and passed
down to Agamemnon by Atreus' brother, Thyestes (*Iliad* 2.100–106).

171 / 159 *you can see his house here, with the double openings* It is dramatically
significant that Philoctetes' cave (which dominates the stage platform)
has two "doors." There might be a revealing parallel to this cave with
two entrances; the cave of the nymphs on the harbor of the sea god
Phorkys on Ithaca also has two entries (*Odyssey* 13.109–12). The entrance facing north is accessible to men; that to the south is reserved
for the gods. As we stage the *Philoctetes*, Herakles appears at the mouth
of the cave not entered by the human actors of the play. (See stage
directions to line 1593/1409.)

193 / 194 *savage-minded Chryse* The accident is referred to again in 1487–90/1327–
28. Chryse is the name both of a place and a minor divinity (apparently
a nymph) associated with the cult of Apollo. The sanctuary of Apollo
at "sea-girt Chryse" was on a now submerged island off the northeast
coast of Lemnos, where there was also a shrine of Chryse. Pausanias,
who wrote a *Description of Greece* around the middle of the second
century A.D., records the sinking of the island (8.33.4).

197 / 199–200 *the time when it is determined that Troy must be destroyed* The proph-
ecies concerning the crucial role of Philoctetes and his bow in the fall
of Troy are first revealed by Odysseus (125–27/113–15) and then the
Trader (622–25/603–21). The equally crucial role of Neoptolemos in
the taking of Troy is a part of Neoptolemos' deception of Philoctetes
(345–47/353), and then stated clearly by Neoptolemos as Helenos'
prophecy at the end of the play (1490–1510/1433–39).

SCENE 1 214–393/191–390

234 / 239–40 *I am from the island of Skyros* Neoptolemos' father Achilles came from
Phthia in the plains of Thessaly. Skyros, a small island in the Sporades
between the coast of Thessaly and Troy, was the refuge his mother (or
his mortal father, Peleus) found for her young son in her vain attempt

to avert his destiny. As the grandson of Lykomedes, Neoptolemos succeeded to the kingship of the island.

The name Neoptolemos means "He who is new to war" (*polemos*), In the post-Homeric epic, the *Kypria*, this name was given to him by Achilles' guardian, Phoinix, to signify that, like his father, Neoptolemos would prove "the young fighter" (Pausanias, *Description of Greece* 10.26.4). When Neoptolemos arrives at Troy, the Achaians greet him as an Achilles come back to life (358/357–58).

247 / 249 *How should I know someone I've never seen before?* Nor does Neoptolemos know his father whom he had never seen before. Both Achilles and Philoctetes belong to a vanishing generation of heroes. See the note to line 349/350.

260 / 262 *the master of the arms of Herakles* The bow and arrows given to Philoctetes at the pyre of Herakles on top of Mt. Oita. Some of the booty awarded to Philoctetes by the grateful Greek army is to be dedicated on Mt. Oita as "tribute to my bow" (1623–24/1422–23).

297 / 302 *there's no harbor* There are fine harbors on Lemnos, and in Sophocles' time it was frequently visited by ships from Athens bound for Thrace and the Hellespont. Philoctetes invokes the harbors of the island he is leaving at 1001/936–40.

306 / 307 *But this one thing, when I mention it* The reluctance of the occasional visitors to Lemnos to carry Philoctetes off the island to his home in Malis is simply explained by the fact that he is polluted by his wound. Such pollution (*miasma*) is unlucky for sailors who depend on the winds and the good will of the gods. His cries of agony were ill-omened as the Greeks sacrificed to the gods; Philoctetes explains as much in 1143–64/1031–34.

308 / 311–12 *I am wasting away—for ten years now* The Greek army had been camped before the wall of Troy for ten years after its commanders abandoned Philoctetes on the island on their way there. The period of ten years of warfare before the fall of Troy is recognized in the omen interpreted by Chalkas in *Iliad* 2.311–32 (line 329) and in Aeschylus, *Agamemnon* 40; cf. Euripides, *Electra* 1154 and *Trojan Women* 20.

316 / 321 *the Atreidai and fierce Odysseus* Odysseus is included with the Atreidai as the object of Philoctetes' fierce anger, but Odysseus alone is associated with the threat of violence (*bia*), as he is in 575/592 (where the same

word stands for more than the Homeric periphrasis for the "person" of Odysseus). Philoctetes is scrupulously careful to stress this violence. For his part, Neoptolemos recognizes only the Atreidai as being responsible for the abandonment of Philoctetes. He even refers to Odysseus by the most enobling of his Homeric epithets, *dios* ("godlike"); the alternative would have been the formulaic "son of Laertes" or "man of many wiles" (as in *Odyssey* 1.1). According to the prophecy of Helenos, Philoctetes could be *persuaded* but not forced to leave Lemnos for Troy (624/612). In his only direct encounter with Philoctetes, Odysseus threatens to drive him to Troy "by force" (1450/1297) and in fact has the men from his ship seize him (1102/1003).

332 / 333 *struck down by Apollo* According to the later epic tradition, Achilles was killed by an arrow shot by Paris. But it was Apollo who directed his aim to Achilles' vulnerable heel. (The role of Apollo in Achilles' death is alluded to by the dying and prophetic Hektor in *Iliad* 22.359; cf. 19.416–7). This "double determination" of both human and divine agency is illustrated in the case of the death of Patroklos, who was stunned by Apollo, wounded by the Trojan Euphorbos, and dispatched by Hektor, who takes his arms. But Apollo was ultimately responsible for Patroklos' death (*Iliad* 16.777–815).

343 / 344 *Phoinix, the man who had reared my father* Sophocles composed a *Phoinix*, of which we know very little. Phoinix is best known from his role and speech in the embassy to persuade Achilles to return to battle in *Iliad* 9.432–605. He is accompanied in this embassy by Odysseus and Ajax.

349 / 350 *my longing for the dead man* Neoptolemos has no knowledge of his father, living or dead. In this, he resembles Odysseus' son, Telemachos. Both were conceived as the Greek armies gathered for the Trojan war. Neoptolemos' "longing for the dead man" is a longing whose only real object is the reputation (*kleos*) of his father.

355 / 355 *Sigeion* "Hateful Sigeion" is a strategic city on the Dardanelles, which had been an Athenian possession since it was annexed by Miltiades the younger at the beginning of the fifth century. It is hateful because the tomb of Achilles was located there, near the city of Ilion. Here Alexander of Macedon honored Achilles when he crossed into Asia, Plutarch, *Life of Alexander* 15.

362 / 362 *my father's weapons* One set of Achilles' arms were worn by Patroklos as he entered battle as a surrogate of Achilles and stripped from him by

Apollo; they were taken by Hektor and recovered from Hektor's body by Achilles (*Iliad* 16.130–39, 792–804, and 17.191). The other set was divine and the work of Hephaistos fashioned to replace these as Achilles returns to battle. They are described in *Iliad* 18.468–614. This divine armor was the object of the contention between Odysseus and Ajax for the arms of Achilles and the arms Sophocles brings to mind.

CHORAL INTERLUDES 394–401/391–402 AND 518–25/507–18

This short choral song is the first *stasimon*, or song sung in the orchestra after the entry of the chorus. It is answered by its companion piece at 518–25. The chorus of soldiers from Skyros invoke the Phrygian goddess Kybele, the Anatolian Earth Mother or Mother of the Gods. As the mother of Zeus, she was recognized by the Greeks as Rhea, but she also had a cult as the Mother of the Gods. She had an important cult on Lemnos. The chorus invoke the Mother, but ask nothing of her. Neoptolemos' sailors are willing participants in the fiction Neoptolemos rehearses to Philoctetes as they recall the fictive prayer they made at Troy to this awesome foreign goddess on the occasion of the award of the arms of Achilles to Odysseus. Her cult stronghold was on Mt. Ida above Troy. Her power extended from Troy to the south to Lydia and Sardis, a city watered by the Paktolos, a river with deposits of gold. Kybele is represented in art and literature as being drawn in her chariot by lions.

402–54 / 403–52 Philoctetes, who has been virtually without human contact for ten years, questions Neoptolemos about the warriors who sailed to Troy: Achilles, Patroklos, the "greater" Ajax (the son of Telamon), and the young son of Nestor, Antilochos. All are dead and all were seen by Odysseus in Hades (*Odyssey* 11.465–72). Three were killed in the fighting at Troy; Ajax committed suicide on the shore of the Troad. This interview in the *Philoctetes* is Sophocles' tragic counterpart of the interview of Odysseus with the comrades who fell in Troy in the Book of the Dead of the *Odyssey* (the Nekyia of book 11). But in this list of Greek warriors, the survivors—Odysseus, his close companion, Diomedes, and the "ugliest" of the Achaians, Thersites—are all base. As Neoptolemos says: "war never chooses to take the disgraceful man, but will always prefer those who are most noble" (436–37/436–37). Neoptolemos makes no mention of the suicide of Ajax.

414 / 417 *Odysseus, begot by Sisyphos and sold to Laertes* In a form of the legend of Odysseus that surfaces after Homer's *Odyssey*, Odysseus' mother, An-

tikleia was made pregnant by the wily Sisyphos, King of Corinth. She was bought with a bride price (*edna*) by Odysseus' presumed father, Laertes. Significantly, this genealogy comes from Aeschylus' *Contest over the Arms*, fr. 175 Radt. In the *Odyssey*, by contrast, his lineage is taken back to the trickster Autolykos (*Odyssey* 19.394), who in one tradition matched wits with Sisyphos.

442 / 442 *Not him, but a certain Thersites* This is the sharpest barb cast at Odysseus in the *Philoctetes*. It sticks. In the *Iliad*, Thersites is described as the ugliest of the Greeks who came to Troy. He rises to speak against Agamemnon before the full assembly of the Achaians. For his boldness and effrontery (his name means brazen), he is beaten by Odysseus to the delight of the army (*Iliad* 2.243–77). Yet Homer admits that Thersites was an appealing speaker (*Iliad* 2.246).

453–54 / 451–52 *in looking upon matters divine, I find the gods themselves are evil* Philoctetes' dark assessment of the gods who allow men like Odysseus to remain alive changes as he hears Herakles address him at the end of the play. And in the immediate sequel he will invoke "suppliant Zeus" to persuade Neoptolemos to take him off the island (**484/494**).

494 / 484 *suppliant Zeus* Zeus *hikesios*, the god who protects suppliants (*hiketai*) who have no other guarantee of protection.

503–7 / 494–99 This passage acknowledges the rare human contact Philoctetes has with sailors who refuse to take him on board. Skyros lies to the southwest of Lemnos; Chalkodon (evidently a city on the island of Euboia) is a reminiscence of a line in the Catalogue of Ships (*Iliad* 2.540), where the leader of the Euboean contingent is said to be the "son of Chalkodon." There is no Chalkodon known on the island, and Chalkodon is probably Sophocles' archaism for the city of Chalkis. The Spercheios is the major river of Malis.

548 / 542 *Son of Achilles* The actor who also plays the part of Odysseus enters the stage. He is disguised as a trader. He presents the second of the lying tales by which Odysseus hopes to convince Philoctetes to sail to Troy. Again the theme of deception (*dolos*) surfaces in the play. In this case, deception is a matter of disguise as well as lies. In disguising a member of the crew of Neoptolemos' ship as a merchant captain—merchants were sacred to Hermes the "trickster" (*dolios*)—Odysseus replicates his own history of disguise as he penetrated Troy dressed in rags with lash marks upon his body (the tale of Helen in *Odyssey* 4.244–50). With

Diomedes, he takes a notorious part in the night ambush of Dolon in the episode known as the Doloneia (*Iliad* 10). His feined madness before arriving at Troy, his disguises at Troy, and his strategem of the Trojan horse all prepare for his disguises and anonymity as he returns to Ithaca and remains there in disguise. He even continues to conceal his identity after the killing of the suitors of Penelope as he is reunited with his aged father, Laertes (*Odyssey* 24.303–14).

553 / 549 *Peparethos*   Now the island of Skopelos in the Sporades to the south and west of Lemnos.

565 / 562 *They have gone in pursuit of you—Phoinix, and the sons of Theseus*   All of these embassies following on the death of Achilles are reenactments of the embassy of Odysseus, Ajax, and Phoinix to Achilles in book 9 of the *Iliad*. They figured in the tradition of the Epic Cycle. The embassy of Diomedes to Lemnos figures in *The Little Iliad*; that of the sons of Theseus in *The Sack of Troy*.

567 / 563 *To bring me back with violence, or with words?*   Neoptolemos' question reflects what seems to have been an essential condition in Helenos' prophecy concerning the taking of Troy: Philoctetes would have to be *persuaded* to come to Troy. The alternative to persuasion (words, *logoi*) is *bia* (force). Later in the play Odysseus' men actually seize Philoctetes by force (1102/1003).

611 / 601 *What can they be longing for?*   The question and the word *pothos* (a longing for something absent) recall the language of the *Iliad* and the prediction that the day will come when the Greek army at Troy comes to *miss* Achilles and *remember* Philoctetes long out of mind (*Iliad* 1.240 and 2.716–20), just as they recall Neoptolemos' longing for his father, **349/350**.

615 / 606 *Helenos*   The Trojan augur, Helenos, figures in the *Iliad* (6.76 and 576). In the post-Homeric tradition, Helenos was forced by Odysseus to reveal the fate of Troy. In the *Philoctetes*, his contingent prophecy concerning the combination of forces necessary to the destruction of Troy must be pieced together from the deceptive speech of the Trader (**613–29/603–12**) and Neoptolemos' honest words at the end of the play (**1499–1510/1336–47**). Neoptolemos must be brought from Skyros to Troy; Philoctetes, from Lemnos, willingly and with his bow. At Troy Philoctetes' injured foot will be healed either by the brothers Machaon and Podaleirios, the doctors of the Greek camp, or by Asklepios himself

(1630/1437). Philoctetes will then kill Paris, and Neoptolemos will play his part in sack of the city that had withstood ten years of siege. This much is not a part of Odysseus' deceit; its truth is authoritatively confirmed by Herakles in 1611–32/1421–44. Helenos survives the fall of Troy. His destiny is to marry Hector's widow, his sister-in-law, Andromache (Euripides, *Andromache* 1243–47) and greet Aeneas with another prophecy on Aeneas' way to Italy from Buthrotum in northwest Greece (Vergil, *Aeneid* 3.293–355).

616–17 / 607–8 *Odysseus, who is called every foul and insulting name* Just as he can bear the anonymity of disguise, Odysseus can bear the insults he instructs his confederates to heap upon him in the presence of Philoctetes. His instructions to Neoptolemos are the same (73–74/64–65). In Euripides' *Philoctetes*, he is called "the common plague of all of Greece" (Dio, *Speech* 59 §8).

619 / 606 *coming upon him alone and at night* Odysseus' capture of Helenos at night is meant to recall the night expedition he and Diomedes made against Troy (*Iliad* 10) and their capture of the unwary Dolon and to foreshadow the night in which Troy would be taken.

639 / 639 *like his father* Meaning not Laertes but Sisyphos, who persuaded his wife not to give him the proper mourning ritual in death and then persuaded Persephone, the goddess of the Underworld, to release him from Hades to return to life and punish his wife. See the note to 414/417.

669 / 654 *And what is it you're holding now?* It is only at this point of the action that Philoctetes appears with his great bow in hand. Now begins what has been called "the sacrament of the bow."

689 / 670 *a kindness* The kindness of agreeing to put a torch to Herakles' funeral pyre.

690 / 671 *I don't regret . . . having you as a friend* Neoptolemos' words in Greek seem to reflect the meaning of Philoctetes' name as Sophocles understood it: "acquiring a friend." It is a compound of *philos* and the verb *ktasthai*, to gain.

CHORAL SONG 696–751/675–729

This is the only full choral song (or regular *stasimon*) of this, the most unlyrical of Sophocles' extant tragedies. It consists of two turns and returns of the chorus (*strophe* and *antistrophe*). The fate of Philoctetes and his abandonment as a cripple on an uninhabited island is something for which the chorus of islanders can find no parallel in Greek tradition and no example in their own experience. The inappropriateness of the parallel the chorus seeks in the punishment of Ixion simply stresses Philoctetes' isolation. His life on Lemnos is shared by no human companion; his fate is without precedent in the legends that fill the choral odes of Greek tragedies.

Ixion was a king of Thessaly, who had murdered his father-in-law. Absolved of the stain of homicide by Zeus, the ingrate attempted to seduce Hera. Zeus frustrated this rape by substituting a cloud for his wife and punished Ixion with the torment of being bound to a wheel that turned perpetually. Philoctetes had committed no such offense, but had rather lived a just life (704–5/680–85). Yet his fate was to hear the ceaseless roar of the sea without a companion to bring him medicinal herbs or respond to his cries of agony (as the chorus does now). Only the echoing cliffs respond to him (1655–60/1458–60). Without grain or wine, the hunter Philoctetes is reduced to the most primitive form of human life. (Fishing seems out of the question for a Homeric hero.) Even the thought of returning to his father's estate takes his imagination to the mountain nymphs of Malis, the banks of the Spercheios, and the slopes of Oita. The mention of Mt. Oita and Herakles' self-immolation there prepares for the long scene of the crisis of the wound to Philoctetes' foot. This scene both parallels and follows the scene of Herakles' suffering from the shirt poisoned by the blood of the centaur Nessos staged in Sophocles' *The Women of Trachis* (983–1043).

790 / 762–63 *But take the bow* In his paroxym of pain, Philoctetes entrusts his bow to the care of Neoptolemos, first asking him to worship the formidable weapon to avert the divine jealousy (*phthonos*) that had pursued their first possessor, Herakles, and then continued to pursue Philoctetes on Lemnos. Earlier, Neoptolemos had asked to hold and worship Philoctetes' bow "as I would a god" (673/657).

834–85 / 791–94 *Son . . . take me up and burn me in the fire called Lemnian* There is no active volcano on Lemnos, but the expression Lemnian fire was proverbial and referred to the vulcanism of a mountain known as Moschylos. This is one of the reasons the god Hephaistos was associated with the island, cf. 1079/986.

823–26 / 791–94 *Odysseus . . . Agamemnon, Menelaos* Even as the bow is transferred to Neoptolemos, Philoctetes would transfer his agony to the Greeks he considers responsible for his abandonment on Lemnos. Elsewhere in the play, Agamemnon and Menelaos are referred to as "the sons of Atreus" (Atreidai) to stress their criminal parentage.

835–39 / 799–803 Philoctetes asks Neoptolemos to perform the same service he had performed for Herakles on Mt. Oita, when he consented to put the torch to his funeral pyre. Neoptolemos' reaction is that of Herakles' son, Hyllos, who refused the request. Philoctetes' request seems to carry the promise that Neoptolemos too will receive the bow as a reward for his services.

856 / 814 *Up* —Before Philoctetes falls asleep in a state of exhaustion, he attempts to ask Neoptolemos to help him return to the protection of his cave. Neoptolemos, who fails to understand, thinks he is looking up to the sky. Sophocles' gesture of drawing the attention of his audience "up" prepares for the epiphany of Herakles at what we argue is the "divine" entrance to Philoctetes' cave (1599/1409; see the note to 171). As it is, Philoctetes collapses before he can return to his cave.

CHORAL SONG 873–913/827–64

The lyrics of the chorus have two motivations: in the strophe they attempt to lull Philoctetes to sleep and, as they are addressed to Neoptolemos in the antistrophe, to move him to take Philoctetes' bow and sail away with Odysseus to Troy. The favorable breeze, like Philoctetes' helpless sleep, gives Neoptolemos and his crew the occasion to accomplish their mission with Odysseus' sure approval. In the *Iliad*, Hera travels from Olympos to Lemnos where she finds Sleep (Hypnos) and Death (Thanatos), 14.230–31.

995 / 931 *In seizing my bow, you have snatched, too, my life* Sophocles connects the words bow (*toxa*) and life (*bíos*) here and elsewhere in the play. He seems to have in mind a saying of Heraclitus that connects the word bow (*biós*) with the word for life: "Life is the name of the bow; its work death," Herakleitos 22 B fr. 48 in Diels-Kranz, *Die Fragmente der Vorsokratiker* (Berlin 1951). The same association recurs in **1239/1126**, where the bow is called "my means of living."

1012 / 941–42 *the sacred bow of Herakles* Sacred because it once belonged not to a hero, who is the son of Zeus, but a *heros* who has become one of the immortals gods on Olympos. In the Book of the Dead of the *Odyssey*, Odysseus reports that he saw the terrifying shade (as opposed to the Olympian presence) of Herakles, armed with this strung bow, ready to release his deadly arrows (*Odyssey* 11.601–8).

1135–36 / 1026–27 *I . . . willingly sailed as captain of seven ships* Unlike either Achilles or Odysseus, Philoctetes sailed toward Troy as a willing participant in the expedition. See the note to line 79/72 and Aeschylus, *Agamemnon* 841.

1145 / 1032–33 *How will you be able to burn sacrifices* The excuse given by the leaders of the Greek army for leaving Philoctetes on Lemnos was religious: the offense of his wound and cries of agony would disturb their worship of the gods. This religious pretext is no longer compelling, once the Greeks need Philoctetes and his bow. A passage from Thucydides' *The Peloponnesian War* makes it clear what the inhibitions of an army setting out to invade a foreign land would have been. In describing the launching of the Athenian armada against Sicily in the summer of 415, Thucydides evokes the trumpet signal enjoining absolute silence on the army before the offering of prayer and libations, 6.31.5.

1174 / 1057 *After all, Teucer is with us* Odysss pretends that he can manage without Philoctetes himself and use his bow without him. Both Teucer, Ajax's brother and the renowned archer of *Iliad* 13.313, and Odysseus himself can manage the bow. In the games on the island of Skeria, Odysseus professes expertise as an archer (*Odyssey* 8.215–20), yet acknowledges Philoctetes' superiority "when we Achaians fought as archers in the land of Troy" (219–20). Odysseus' mastery of the bow is most impressively demonstrated in the revenge he takes on the suitors in *Odyssey* 21 and 22. Teucer has a dubious part to play in the events following the death of Achilles. In Sophocles' *Ajax*, Ajax abuses him as "archer" (1120), and in one tradition (the fiction of the orator Alkidamas' *Against Palamedes*) it was Teucer who shot an arrow into the Trojan camp carrying the forged message with which Odysseus incriminated Palamedes of collaboration with the enemy.

1183 / 1063–64 *adorned in weapons that are mine* The bite of the sarcasm is that Odysseus needs weapons that are all show and disguise his real cowardice, as was the case of the arms of Achilles he won by eloquence and not as a prize for his valor.

PHILOCTETES' LYRIC MONODY 1200–1344/1081–1217

This long passage of formal lamentation (*kommós*) is in form a lyric exchange between Philoctetes, who is the only actor on the stage, and the chorus. It is not a true exchange until Philoctetes finally responds to the chorus in 1288/1170. It is composed of two strophes and antistrophes and concludes by an epode (of a variety of meters). It prepares for yet stands in subtle contrast to Philoctetes' last words of farewell to the island where he spent ten years in pain and isolation, 1647–71/1452–68. In his last evocation of the island, the island becomes sacred and the haunt of gods. In this dirge of lamentation, Philoctetes first imagines himself abandoned once again and without his bow (in the first strophe) and then, suddenly, he turns in imagination to the sight of Odysseus, seated on the shore, exulting in the possession of the bow of Herakles (in the antistrophe).

1331 / 1210 *That I might see again my father* Philoctetes' desire to join his father in Hades is more than a symptom of his despair with his life; he wants to return to an earlier and better generation.

1467 / 1312–13 *Achilles, who held the greatest nobility* Philoctetes' generous praise of Achilles and his nobility both in life and in death deliberately recalls Odysseus' praise of Achilles' power over the dead in Hades. It also recalls Achilles' curt rejection of the notion of there being any consolation of lordship in death: "I would rather serve on the plot of a poor farmer with no land of his own than be king over all the dead who have perished!" (*Odyssey* 11.484–91).

1494 / 1333 *the sons of Asklepios* These are Machaon and Podaleirios, physicians in the army of the Achaeans, who cured Philoctetes' wound on his arrival at Troy. At the end of the play, Herakles says that Asklepios himself will heal Philoctetes' wounds (1630/1437), which amounts to the same thing.

1629 / 1436 *as two lions that feed together* In the *Iliad* the simile describes Odysseus and Diomedes as they set out in their nocturnal mission against Troy (10.297). This episode gives the simile here a sinister connotation.

1631–32 / 1439–40 *once again, the city is to be taken by my bow* A reference to the first Greek expedition against the Troy of Laomedon a generation before. It included Herakles, Telamon, father of Ajax, and Philoctetes.

1633 / 1440–41 *But remember, when you conquer the land* Herakles' warning to Philoctetes and Neoptolemos casts an ugly shadow over the divinely imposed solution to the fated capture and sack of Troy. It seems to echo the warning of Clytemnestra in Aeschylus' *Agamemnon* against the victorious Greek army's sacrilegous treatment of the altars and temples of the gods of Troy (*Agamemnon* 338–42; cf. 527–28) and the similar warning of King Darius in Aeschylus' *Persians* to respect the shrines of the Greek gods, a warning his son Xerxes did not heed (*Persians* 800–17). The events following the capture of Troy are well known from the poems of the Epic Cycle (*The Fall of Troy* and Lesches of Mytilene's *Little Iliad*) and from two plays of Euripides especially, the *Hecuba* (where they are recalled in 523–68) and *Andromache*. Neoptolemos, the noble son of Achilles in Sophocles' *Philoctetes*, becomes the bloodthirsty Pyrrhos (so well known from Vergil, *Aeneid* 2.526–58), whose savage bloodlust was already commemorated by Polygnotos on the walls of the club house of the Knidians at Delphi. He is held responsible for the murder of Priam at the altar of Zeus in his courtyard and (in the lyric poet Ibycus) of Priam's daughter Polyxena. Ajax, son of Oileus, attempted to rape Cassandra in the temple of Athena, and Odysseus and Diomedes carried off Athena's cult statue, the Palladion. Pindar explained Pyrrhos' murder at Delphi as motivated by the anger of Apollo over his crimes at Troy (*Paean* 6.98–120).

1647–71 / 1452–68 In Philoctetes' final farewell to Lemnos, the island has become "divine" as Homer had described it (*Iliad* 21.79). As Philoctetes leaves it, its nymphs, Hermes, and Apollo take possession of it.

GLOSSARY

ACHAIANS: A generic name for the Greek forces who made the expedition against Troy.

ACHILLES: Son of Peleus and Thetis and, while alive, counted as "best of the Achaians." He was the father of Neoptolemos. He was killed by an arrow directed by Apollo and Paris.

AGAMEMNON: Son of Atreus, brother of Menelaos, king of Argos, and leader of the second Greek expedition against Troy.

AJAX: Son of Telamon of Salamis. He lost to Odysseus in the contest for the arms of Achilles and committed suicide.

ANTILOCHOS: Son of Nestor of Pylos, killed in the Trojan War.

APOLLO: Son of Zeus and Leto, an archer god, responsible for the death of Achilles.

ARGIVES: A generic name for the Greeks who made the expedition against Troy.

ASKLEPIOS: The Greek god of healing who is to cure Philoctetes' wound.

ATHENA: The virgin daughter of Zeus and patroness of Athens and Odysseus.

ATREIDAI: The sons of Atreus, Agamemnon and Menelaos.

CHALKODON: A city on the island of Euboia, probably Sophocles' invention.

CHRYSE: A now submerged island of the northeast coast of Lemnos; also a minor goddess associated with the sanctuary of Apollo on the island.

DEIDAMIA: Daughter of King Lykomedes of Skyros and mother of Neoptolemos by Achilles.

DIOMEDES: One of the most prominent Greek warriors at Troy; accompanied Odysseus on the night raid against Troy.

EUBOIA: A large island off the east coast of Boeotia.

HADES: Brother of Zeus and Poseidon, god of the Underworld. Also the Underworld itself.

HELENOS: Son of Priam and the prophet who, captured by Odysseus, is forced to reveal the secret of Troy's capture.

HERAKLES: The son of Zeus and Alcmene, who accompanied Philoctetes on the first Greek expedition to Troy and gave him his bow in thanks for his putting a torch to his funeral pyre. He is worshipped both as an Olympian god and a mortal *heros*.

HERMES: The son of Zeus and the Arcadian nymph, Maia. He is addressed as the god of guile.

HESPHAISTOS: The god associated with vulcanism and metalworking who gave his name to Hephaistia, one of the two important cities of Lemnos.

IXION: Absolved by Zeus for murder of a kinsman, he attempted to rape Hera. His punishment was being bound to a perpetually rotating wheel.

LEMNOS: An important island between mainland Greece and Troy associated with Hephaistos.

LYKOMEDES: King of Skyros, father of Deidamia, and grandfather of Neoptolemos. Neoptolemos succeeds him as king.